William H. P. Hatch

MUNERA STUDIOSA

EDITED BY

MASSEY HAMILTON SHEPHERD, JR.

AND

SHERMAN ELBRIDGE JOHNSON

WITH A PREFACE BY

HENRY BRADFORD WASHBURN

WIPF & STOCK · Eugene, Oregon

Wipf and Stock Publishers
199 W 8th Ave, Suite 3
Eugene, OR 97401

Munera Studiosa
By Shepherd, Massey Hamilton, JR. and Johnson, Sherman Elbridge
ISBN 13: 978-1-5326-0867-4
Publication date 9/30/2016
Previously published by The Episcopal Theological School, 1946

These studies are presented to the Reverend William Henry Paine Hatch, Ph.D., D.D., D.Théol., Edmund Swett Rousmaniere Professor of the Literature and Interpretation of the New Testament in the Episcopal Theological School, on the occasion of his seventieth birthday, as a token of affection and gratitude, by his friends

CONTENTS

	PAGE
PREFACE	vii

HENRY BRADFORD WASHBURN, *Episcopal Theological School*

I. THE PSALMS 3
CHARLES LINCOLN TAYLOR, JR., *Episcopal Theological School*

II. A TWICE-BURIED APOCALYPSE 23
CHARLES CUTLER TORREY, *Yale University*

III. SUPERFLUOUS ΚΑΊ IN THE LORD'S PRAYER AND ELSEWHERE 41
HENRY JOEL CADBURY, *Harvard University*

IV. THE SOURCES OF PAULINE MYSTICISM . . 49
CHESTER CHARLTON MCCOWN, *Pacific School of Religion*

V. POST-PAULINE PAULINISM 69
BURTON SCOTT EASTON, *General Theological Seminary*

VI. A VENTURE IN THE SOURCE ANALYSIS OF ACTS 91
MASSEY HAMILTON SHEPHERD, JR., *Episcopal Theological School*

VII. A SUBSIDIARY MOTIVE FOR THE WRITING OF THE DIDACHE 107
SHERMAN ELBRIDGE JOHNSON, *Episcopal Theological School*

VIII. ARCHAIC CRUCIFIXION ICONOGRAPHY . . 123
HAROLD RIDEOUT WILLOUGHBY, *University of Chicago*

IX. NOTES ON BOOK-BURNING 145
ARTHUR STANLEY PEASE, *Harvard University*

CONTENTS

X. RELIGION AND POETRY 161
FREDERICK CLIFTON GRANT, *Union Theological Seminary*

BIBLIOGRAPHY OF THE WRITINGS OF WILLIAM HENRY PAINE HATCH 179
Compiled by Professor Hatch

PREFACE

Henry Bradford Washburn

Episcopal Theological School

Dr. Hatch knows the contributors to the present volume too well to look upon the gift as *signum senectutis incipientis*.

He also knows his Scriptures so thoroughly that he is not inclined to take the Psalmist over-seriously when he says that "the days of our years are three score and ten," and then goes on to forecast something of the labor and sorrow before "we fly away."

He will discover in the following pages gifts from those who are familiar with his years of quiet and thorough preparation for a Ministry of devotion and scholarship, and who know his worth as minister, teacher, scholar and author and who respect and honor him with steadily increasing power. They are now counting on him to continue to be just what he has been as he goes forward to the no less productive years that lie ahead.

Trained and disciplined in modern languages, equally well trained and disciplined in the classics, adding to these the mastery of other languages necessary to the understanding of Biblical linguistic usage, sensitive to the meaning of words, Dr. Hatch has made himself a student before he has allowed himself to become a teacher or to remain as one. He has shown us that the teacher who is always ready to be taught, who, however confident he may be of the conclusions he has reached, always leaves a window open for fresher air and brighter light, is alone the helpful teacher, the productive scholar.

Such conditions of learning, and others equally essential, he has carried into the class-room. He has encouraged a similar mental attitude among his students, hoping that all would value careful foundation-laying and continuously careful building. He may have been a little over-hopeful that all of his students might become masters of the Greek text of the New Testament. Nevertheless, he has impressed his men with the value of thoroughness; he has sent out into the Ministry men impatient with guess-work and superficiality — men ready to turn to those who can tell them the truth.

While he has been setting an example of scholarly purpose in the class-room he has been making his contribution to policies of theological education. In his quiet, tranquil, deliberate manner he has taken an active part in discussions relative to the improvement of present conditions, standing firmly for the admission into theological schools of those only who are sufficiently prepared; giving degrees to those only who show attainment and promise; exposing the students, preferably in a university neighborhood, "foursquare to all the 'academic' winds that blow." From the opening of his active association with educational problems down to the present moment there has been a fine consistency in these ideas of his. It has had its beneficent effect.

His serene, honest, thorough and useful contribution to theological education has not been cloistered. He has honored not only himself but his friends, his schools and his university by a wider field of service. In his Sabbatical leaves of absence he has sought and enjoyed the friendship of scholars of many countries; he has shared in their scholarly reflections. He is at home in the libraries of the world; he knows their librarians. He is more familiar than many a native with the Egyptian and Palestinian holy places. He is in sympathetic touch with the English, the Scottish, the French, the German, the oriental mind. He is among friends and colleagues everywhere.

Outward and visible signs of his professional interest and

accomplishment may be found in what he has written. Their quality may be known by the editors and the Foundations that have been proud to sponsor them and by the scholarly welcome they have received. And while some of those who know him best and are familiar with his mastery of the Pauline writings are tempted to paraphrase the ancient servant's daily encouragement in saying "Master, remember the Romans," we recognize his unique contribution to New Testament learning in his successive volumes of study of the New Testament manuscripts. They have already taken their place among indispensable material. They fill a long-felt need in the field of New Testament and paleographical study. They, as well as other products of his sanctum, place him finally among those whose services have proved of permanent value. They have come as tranquilly from his pen as conversation comes from his lips. They have come so gradually and so noiselessly that even those of his inner circle hardly knew of their coming. And now that they are here they need no correction, no improvement.

So much for the present and the past. With such a present and such a past the future will care for itself. Friendships will increase in number and they will deepen. Plans now slowly developing will come to maturity. Ideas born of stimulating association, honest study and research, candid matching of minds and love of the truth, will surely take their shape. And we his friends who honor and love him will honor and love him all the more. We are grateful to him for what he has been and for what he is. We expect to be more grateful still, for he little realizes how much his gentle, strong, intelligent personality directs and rules our hearts.

MUNERA STUDIOSA

THE PSALMS

Charles Lincoln Taylor, Jr.
Episcopal Theological School

As two men were leaving a college chapel some years ago, the younger remarked that the service had consisted almost entirely of psalms. One psalm had been read responsively, another had been used as a canticle, a third had been the inspiration for the hymn, still others had been echoed in the prayer. "For the purposes of worship," replied the elder, "it is difficult to find material better than the psalms."

At least this collection of ancient hymns has mirrored men's deepest gratitude and trust in many parts of the world for over half a hundred generations. It seems to have been an important staple in the spiritual food of Jesus Christ. It provides common ground for the worship not only of many types of Christian, but of Christians with Jews. Calvin called it "the soul's anatomy"; others have found it "the heart of the Bible," "the Bible within the Bible," and the world's greatest devotional literature. When one book of the Old Testament is bound with the New, it is the Psalms.

The object of this essay, for all the dangers of a brief summary, is to tell why the psalms merit these distinctions.

I

In part the hold of this literature is its commanding poetic beauty. Its words are living words, so full of life that "if you cut them, they bleed."[1]ABstractions are few. Vivid pictures leap from the page to the mind's eye, to its delight.

[1] Cf. J. L. Lowes, "The Noblest Monument of English Prose," *Essays in Appreciation* (Boston, 1936), pp. 3-31.

For simple, pictorial language, the psalms might seem to be at a disadvantage when compared with other parts of the Bible, because psalms are not narratives, nor epic poetry, but, in the main, lyrics. But even in the most prosaic sections of the Psalter this genius for expressing thought concretely appears. "The proud have smeared falsehood over me." [2] "I am become like a bottle in the smoke," — the sooty wineskin hung up under the roof.[3] If such flashes of imagination characterize even the didactic psalms, how much more do the best collections abound in unforgettable pictures. "Deep calleth unto deep." [4] "Righteousness and peace have kissed each other." [5] "If I take the wings of the morning";[6] "With thee is the fountain of life." [7]

Perhaps the two collections which surpass all the others in grace of language and sustained elevation are the Korahite sections, 42–49, 84–89, and the so-called "Songs of Ascents," 120–134. Let memory play upon those Songs of Ascents for a moment for their use of everyday incidents, and for the way in which homely words may express the most sublime truths. Deliverance is like that of a "bird escaped from the snare of the fowler." Joy makes the singers as "those that dream"; those who trust in the Lord are as unshakable as Mount Zion; God's blessing descends "like the dew of Hermon." Children born before the parents are old are "as arrows in the hand of a warrior." Trustful hope is like that of a maid looking to the hand of her mistress. The wife of the pious shall be as a fruitful vine, his children as young olive shoots. God's renewed favor is symbolized by the streams in the South, empty in summer, but full when the rain returns. The persecution of the wicked is like the plowing of furrows upon their victim's

---

[2] Ps. 119:69.
[3] Ps. 119:83.
[4] Ps. 42:7.
[5] Ps. 85:10.
[6] Ps. 139:9.
[7] Ps. 36:9.

back, but the worth of these evil men is no more than the casual grass that grows and dies upon the housetops. On the other hand, "they that sow in tears shall reap in joy." "More than watchmen for the morning" men wait for the Lord. As the mountains surround Jerusalem, so the Lord's care encircles His people. Such is some, though by no means all, of the imagery packed into about one hundred lines of poetry. By handy and simple metaphors, this psalmist provides classic expressions for truths that are permanent and universal, and so enters the ranks of great literary artists. As in *Pilgrim's Progress*, the route to the delectable mountains leads through common everyday experiences.

II

The student of this literature is easily drawn into a number of interesting though somewhat technical questions, such as the form of Hebrew poetry, the occasions for the composition of psalms, and their date. Unfortunately the problem of the nature of Hebrew meter has by no means found any solution that can command general agreement. The essence of the rhythm is a balance of accented syllables between the two parts that make up a line of poetry. There are no measures, no feet, no counting of syllables, but only periods of time marked off against like periods by the same number of accents, or by a second half-line which has one less accent than the first and then a rest. Are the most frequent arrangements four accents followed by four, or four by three, and not three-three and three-two, as is often assumed? At least supplementary accents are a characteristic of poetry in general, and there are many lines which cannot easily be read as three-three and three-two. Is it justifiable to assume a change in meter at these points? [8]

[8] Cf. W. R. Arnold, "The Rhythms of the Ancient Hebrews," *Old*

Were some of the psalms written in strophes? According to Professor Torrey, who is clearly right, "Hebrew poetry in general is not strophic; and even the Psalter contains comparatively few poems made up of stanzas of equal length."[9] Psalms 42–43, however,[10] are a thirty line poem with a recurring refrain at the end of each third, and Psalm 80 may originally have had five stanzas with the same refrain, "Turn us again, O God (*or*, Lord), and cause thy face to shine and we shall be saved," at every fourth line. In general, longer Hebrew poems are written in easily remembered numbers of lines, 20, 22, 30, 40, 70, or 100, while shorter psalms are frequently eight or ten lines long, which was perhaps just the width of a MS. roll.[11]

Are the psalms liturgies, poems that for the most part were composed to accompany cultic acts, and therefore to be understood only in the light of the Temple with its ritual or the practices of the shrines of pre-exilic Israel?[12] Although there is clearly much in the psalms to support this thesis, there are also psalms, such as 119, that are not liturgies; many are better understood as written for private devotion, and imaginative reconstructions of the acts sup-

---

Testament and Semitic Studies in Memory of William Rainey Harper (Chicago, 1908), I, 165–204; and W. H. Cobb, *Criticism of Systems of Hebrew Metre* (Oxford, 1905).

[9] C. C. Torrey, "The Archetype of Psalms 14 and 53," *Journal of Biblical Literature XLVI* (1927), 191.

[10] Omitting Ps. 42:4a and Ps. 42:8.

[11] Occasional light may be thrown on the text by the assumption that the width of a MS. roll was sufficient for some such number of lines. For example, in the alphabetic Psalm 37, verses 7, 20, and 34 each lack a half-line; verses 14, 25, and 40 have a half-line too much. Material from one column crept over into another. Other difficulties of this psalm are explained by writing it in eight line columns and studying the meeting points.

[12] Cf. H. Gunkel, "The Poetry of the Psalms," in D. C. Simpson (ed.), *Old Testament Essays*, 1927; J. P. Peters, *The Psalms as Liturgies* (New York, 1922); S. Waddy, *Homes of the Psalms* (London, 1928); and F. James, *Thirty Psalmists* (New York, 1938).

THE PSALMS 7

posed to lie behind Psalms 84 or 116, for example, easily outstrip all evidence. The assumption that a number of psalms [13] were written to be sung at a supposed New Year festival in honor of the accession of Yahweh to his throne, dramatically represented by the ascent of the king to a throne upon earth, unhappily rests upon no shred of definite contemporary evidence of such a festival in Israel.[14]

As to the date, there is general agreement among scholars that the Psalter is a "collection of collections of psalms," or an anthology of hymns composed and used at various periods of Israelite history. No such unanimity exists over the questions as to how much of the Psalter dates from preexilic times and as to whether there are psalms in this collection from as late as the second century B.C. But the fact that the Pentateuch gives little or no evidence of interest in the Temple music, which is so important for the Chronicler, points to the years 400–250 B.C. as an all-important period for the production of psalms. Further, the comparison between the psalms and the early and late poetry of other parts of the Bible [15] shows that in prolixity of style, in language, and in ideas, the major portion of the psalms belongs with the latter, not the former. On the other point, at how late a date contributions were made to this collection, was there an hiatus in psalm production between the end of the Persian period or even the time of Ben Sira and the Psalms of Solomon, which incidentally bear strong resemblances to the canonical Psalter? And various close connections between the psalms and the literature of the second

---

[13] *E.g.* 47, 93, 96–99.
[14] Cf. S. Mowinckel, *Psalmenstudien* (Kristiania, 1922), II, and for his views in English, C. C. Keet, *A Liturgical Study of the Psalter* (London, 1928).
[15] *E.g.*, with Judges 5, 2 Sam. 1:17ff., and other poems up to the 100 line work of Nahum at the end of the seventh century on the one hand, and with Tobit 13, Judith 16, and the poems of Ben Sira or Luke 1 on the other.

century B.C. point toward the conclusion that there are in the Psalter second century psalms.[16]

III

The reason for the hold of the psalms on men's hearts, however, is neither the many avenues of fruitful and even exciting research they provide scholars, nor their literary form. A sound definition of great literature includes not only worthy expression, but also universal and permanent truth expressed. The value of the psalms is greater in what they say than in the way they say it.

Not that everything said in the psalms has value for us, or, even, is true. The right use of this literature involves recognition of serious deficiencies in it from a Christian point of view. The major difficulty is probably the large amount of imprecation, which mars even some of the otherwise noblest psalms.[17] No amount of praise to the Hebrews for taking evil seriously can make some of these curses useful to Christians. In a debate in the House of Commons, one member approved of the imprecatory psalms on the ground that it was proper to use them if their hatred were directed toward Germans. Another rose to say that the enemies were only spiritual enemies. Then how, commented Dean Inge, does one dash their children against the stones? There are hymns which drop out of our hymn books, such as these verses from no less a person than Isaac Watts:

> There the dark earth and gloomy shades
> Shall clasp their naked body round,
> And welcome their delicious limbs
> With the cold kisses of the ground.

---

[16] Cf. Pfeiffer, *Introduction to the Old Testament* (New York, 1941), p. 630, for the acrostics of Ps. 2 and Ps. 110 which refer to Jannaeus (103 B.C.) and Simon (141 B.C.). What is the relation between I Macc. 7:17 and Ps. 79:2f., between III Macc. 2:20 and Ps. 79:8, between the *ḥasidim* of psalms (26 times) and the *qaddishin* of Daniel (11 times)? How interpret Ps. 44:22, 74:8, or 122:5?   [17] *E.g.* 36, 139.

THE PSALMS

> Pale death shall riot on their souls,
> Their flesh shall noisome vermin eat,
> The just shall in the morning rise
> And find their tyrants at their feet.[18]

Why not let ancient hymns with similar sentiments or even more direct hatred fall into relative disuse? There is sufficient hatred in the world without the engendering of more.

There are other drawbacks also. The protests of righteousness in certain of the psalms are of a self-congratulatory kind, far from Christian humility. The Pharisee's words of self-congratulation, that he is not as other men are, might well have been reminiscent of Psalm 26: "I have walked in thy truth. I have not sat with vain persons, neither will I go in with dissemblers. I have hated the congregation of evil-doers; and will not sit with the wicked. I will wash mine hands in innocency: so will I compass thine altar, O Lord." Except for a few doubtful passages, there is no hope beyond this life. Suffering is regularly a sign of sin and prosperity of right conduct. In spite of notable exceptions, chief among them Psalm 51, which has been called "perhaps the noblest penitential hymn in all the world," [19] there is little confession of sin and little appreciation of the extent and inwardness of sin. Forgiveness often means little more than a return to health and wealth. When the psalmist says, "I have been young and now am old; yet have I not seen the righteous forsaken, nor his seed begging bread," [20] he seems to us either limited in his experience or forgetful. The families of too many good men are starving in the world today for this kind of dogmatism about the correspondence between virtue and material reward. But

---

[18] Watts, 1707. Quoted in J. M. P. Smith, *The Religion of the Psalms* (Chicago, 1922), p. 4.
[19] The phrase is Montefiore's, *The Bible For Home Reading* (New York, 1901), p. 489.
[20] Ps. 37:25.

if there are these deficiencies and sub-Christian aspects of the psalms, all the more there must be extraordinary merits to enable them to survive and to mean so much to seekers for God. These merits for the most part are not hidden nor subtle. Like hymns generally, the psalms provide an easily grasped and easily remembered statement of the fundamental thoughts and emotions of man toward God. In brief, they are the world's best vehicle of praise and its most valuable treasury of trust.

IV

Not the least of the wonders of the psalms is their abounding joy. The greater part were written when the Jews were under foreign oppression, almost none when the nation could be called prosperous, some when it was in dire straits. "Out of the deep" they cry to the Lord, and then they come up from the deep and stand upon the rock. The mood of depression has neither the last nor the dominant word. It is more than counterbalanced by joy.

One has only to call to mind the more familiar psalms to realize how a joyous tone runs through this book. They begin with the word "blessed" — truly fortunate — they end with a paean of praise. They speak of streams that make glad the city of God, of hills that are girded with joy, of dawn and sunset rejoicing, of men singing to the Lord with a voice of thanksgiving and of serving him with gladness. This joy is not obtained by forgetfulness of sorrow. It is not superficial pleasure. It is the deep satisfaction that belongs to the man who is in right relation to God. When the nations make much ado and the kingdoms are moved, the psalmists on the whole look in the right direction, not inward upon themselves with the self-pity that leads to despair, but outward toward God. God is the central reality of life; by acknowledging this, by thanking Him not only for what He has done but for what He is, these writers find a very present help in trouble and rejoice.

The best hymns, generally speaking, have little exhortation, little preoccupation with the soul of the singer, but much affirmation, with God consistently the chief subject. Here the psalms set the standard. Luther's *Ein' Feste Burg* starts from the opening verse of Psalm 46. Watts' "O God our help in ages past" is based directly upon Psalm 90, which is free, in George Tyrrell's words, from "anthropocentric vanity," and provides "an outlook into those immensities in which our greatest philosophers seem less than chirping grasshoppers." [21] Man can forget to whine when he adores God. "Lift up your heads, O ye gates," "O be joyful in the Lord, all ye lands," "Bless the Lord, O my soul, and forget not all his benefits." If "man's chief end is to glorify God and to enjoy him for ever," these psalmists were not far wide of the mark. They could say with Epictetus, "Were I a nightingale, I would act the part of a nightingale; were I a swan, the part of a swan. But since I am a reasonable creature, it is my duty to praise God. This is my business. I do it. Nor will I ever desert this post, so long as it is permitted me; and I call on you to join in the same song." [22] If man is to draw near to God with a garment of praise, the psalms save him from the reproach of nakedness. And what is better clothing? If he does not learn to praise through these words, how shall he learn at all? "If ye have not been faithful in that which is another's, who will give you that which is your own?" [23]

At least it appears that our Pilgrim forefathers learned gratitude through the help of the psalms. William Bradford's *History* tells of the hardships of that first winter, but

---

[21] M. D. Petre, *Autobiography and Life of George Tyrrell* (New York, 1912), II, p. 10.
[22] *Discourses* I xvi (p. 50, ed. Higginson).
[23] Lk. 16:12.

the hardships are not the last word. He turns to the 107th Psalm to apply it to his own people:

Let them praise the Lord, because he is good,
> and his mercies endure for ever.

Yea, let them which have been redeemed of the Lord,
> show how he hath delivered them from the hand of the oppressor.

When they wandered in the desert wilderness out of the way, and found no city to dwell in,
Both hungry and thirsty,
> their soul was overwhelmed in them.

Let them confess before the Lord his loving kindness,
> and his wonderful works before the sons of men.

The order is not always a feeling of gratitude first, then words to express it; there are times when hearts become grateful as they learn the meaning of another's words. There is not greater value of the psalms than their constant recognition of God. "It is a good thing to give thanks unto the Lord."

Praise and thanks are offered God in the psalms chiefly because of his character and his acts of deliverance or helpfulness to men.

As the heavens form a canopy over the earth,
> his friendship forms a canopy over his worshippers.

As far as the east is from the west,
> so far has he removed from us our transgressions.

As a father takes pity on his children,
> the Lord takes pity.

Protection, forgiveness, fatherly love — for these reasons my soul is to bless the Lord.[24] Or, characteristically in Psalm 30,

I will extol thee, O Lord, for thou hast drawn me up,
> (*i.e.*, like a bucket out of a well.)
>> and not let mine enemies rejoice over me.

O Lord my God, I cried unto thee,
> and thou didst heal me.

---

[24] Ps. 103:11–13.

THE PSALMS

O Lord thou didst bring up my soul from Sheol,
> thou didst revive me from among those going down to the pit.

Sing praises to the Lord, ye his saints,
> and give thanks to his holy name.

Though there be a moment in his anger,
> there is a lifetime in his favor,

In the evening weeping,
> but in the morning a shout of joy.

Nature, like man, is part of God's handiwork and subject to His command, and some of the most beautiful psalms, such as 104 or 19, 65 or 29, extol God's activity in the natural realm. But if the two chief avenues to God are, in Kantian phrase, the "starry heavens above and the moral law within," the Hebrews used the former almost not at all. Their religion was not a philosophy about God built up by reflection upon the order or beauty of the universe; it was a personal experience of God's work in the affairs of men. Their God was not a nature God; he was a clan or national God. They did not speculate about him as ruler of the universe; they enjoyed personal relations with him as their helper and friend.[25] And most of the psalms which show marked interest in external nature, in the opinion of this writer, are either to some extent dependent on the nature hymns of other literatures, Egyptian, Babylonian, Canaanite, such as the Hymn of Akhnaton in the case of Psalm 104, or late psalms after Job and Isaiah 40–66 and other writings had taught the Jews a new interest in young lions and Leviathan.[26] These statements need, perhaps, the

---

[25] Cf. R. H. Pfeiffer, "The Dual Origin of Hebrew Monotheism," *Journal of Biblical Literature* XLVI (1927), 193–206.

[26] a. For the Canaanite hymns of Ras Shamra, and their relation to Psalms 18, 29, 45, 68, 88, 89, cf. W. F. Albright, *Archaeology and the Religion of Israel* (Baltimore, 1942), especially pp. 128f.

b. For a Babylonian Shamash hymn, and its relation to Ps. 19A, cf. D. C. Simpson (ed.), *The Psalmists* (Oxford, 1926), pp. 16f., 162.

support of considerable evidence; if they are true, we do well to be on guard both in our discussions of the theology of the Old Testament (*e.g.* in the case of Amos 4:13, 5:8f., 9:5f.) and in our religious emphases today. The riddle of life is not often solved by reflection upon the external universe. Nature indeed may save a religion from narrowness, teach men of their dependence upon God, and provide a daily universal manifestation of the activity of God. But it is ambiguous. The problem of evil, now as for the psalmist, is too painful until one goes into the sanctuary (Ps. 73:16f.).

V

Another reason for the continuing appeal of the psalms is that the type of religion they represent is so sane and practical. To some it may seem materialistic, although the late Archbishop Temple called Christianity, not Judaism, the most materialistic of all the religions. Some sixty-five psalms refer in one way or another to the Temple, a building of stones and mortar. A material edifice, yes, but a center in which God had particularly revealed himself, a center of national unity through tax and pilgrimage, a constant reminder that though Jewish religion is highly personal, it is rooted in the community. *Die Gemeinde ist das fromme Ich.* If the psalms are now used as aids to private devotion, it is well to remember that their personal piety was firmly grounded in the masonry of the house of God. The music rising before the throne of God is not a solo, but a choir.

---

c. For the 14th cent. B.C. Hymn of Akhnaton, in relation to Ps. 104, cf. D. C. Simpson (ed.), *op. cit.*, pp. 18–21, 177–182.

d. For other Babylonian and Egyptian psalms, cf. W. O. E. Oesterley, *A Fresh Approach to the Psalms* (New York, 1937), pp. 23–35.

e. For the theory that Pss. 88 and 89 are specimens of Edomitic poetry cf. R. H. Pfeiffer, *Introduction to the Old Testament*, p. 21. Zoroastrian influence, maintained by Cheyne and Von Gall, is unlikely.

THE PSALMS

What magnificent expressions of joy in corporate religious practice the Psalter contains!

> Send out thy light and thy truth
> that they may lead me,
> Let them bring me to thy holy hill
> and to thy dwelling,
> That I may come to the altar of the Lord,
> to the God of my joy,
> And rejoice and thank thee upon the lyre,
> O Lord, my God.[27]

So also Psalms 63, 48, or 122 and 100, and especially 84:

> How lovely are thy habitations,
> O Lord of hosts.
> My soul faints with longing
> for the courts of the Lord.
> My mind and body cry out with joy
> to the living God.[28]

Here in this psalm, despite the attractive interpretation of it as a temple processional given by J. P. Peters and Stacy Waddy, it is apparent that the communion with God of which it speaks begins in the Temple but by no means stops there. At least the desire of the small birds for the altars, the springs in the dry valley, the vision of God, the shield, the sun or battlement, all convey and probably were intended to convey much more than a prosaic meaning. In the psalms the national and the spiritual, the temporal and eternal, are most happily combined.

VI

The psalms say less about man in relation to his neighbor than they do about his relation to God. Unless one is accustomed to the conservative piety of hymns, he may even be offended by the lack of social idealism in this literature. For it is the prophets who blaze new trails to

[27] Ps. 43:3f. (corrected text).   [28] Ps. 84:1f.

brotherly action; hymns, which are gauged for the average worshipper and rarely catch up to the boldest thought of their times, are the bulwark of conservative orthodoxy. It is frequently remarked how badly our present day hymns lag behind our current ideals and theology.

But in spite of the fact that the psalms are not a handbook of sociology, not a book on morals, not the oracles of voices crying in the wilderness, they are not without value either for the nourishing of a sense of social responsibility or for the stimulation of social ideals. The "ten commandments of the Psalter," for example,[29] lay down the conditions which man must fulfill in relation to his neighbor to be acceptable to God. Psalm 50, somewhat exceptionally, has all the fire of an Amos or Isaiah, with their hatred of formalism and their insistence on moral conduct. Psalm 101 has often been called a "mirror for magistrates," and Psalm 72 describes the conditions — justice, peace and plenty, help to the poor and the end of oppression — in the age of the Messianic King. Psalm 146 describes God's interest in the various less fortunate classes of society, in which interest, by inference, man is to have a share.

The greatest contribution the psalms make to social welfare is to keep before men's minds that state of society in which a God whose nature is just and loving shall rule. They do not actually use the term "Kingdom of God," but they insist that opposition to the God whose throne is founded on righteousness and justice is disastrous. In days when human beings have been accorded divine honors, the words of Psalm 82 ring with particular pertinence.

The Lord takes his stand in the divine assembly, (*i.e.* of human rulers half-deified)
> judging in the midst of the gods.
How long will you judge unjustly
> and favor the person of the wicked?

[29] Ps. 15.

THE PSALMS

Give justice for the oppressed and fatherless,
    vindicate the poor and those in want.
Deliver the impoverished and the needy,
    rescue them from the hand of the wicked.
They have neither knowledge nor sense
    walking hither and thither in darkness...
I said to myself (*i.e.* I thought) you are divine
    and all of you sons of the Most High.
In truth, none the less, you shall die like men (*i.e.* ordinary men)
    and like any ruler you shall fall.
Arise, O Lord, judge the earth,
    for thou dost sift all the nations.

VII

Apart from their assistance in providing the language of praise, the most important service the psalms render is to express trust. About ninety of the psalms deal in one way or another with trouble, on the edges or in the heart of the problem of reconciling the evil and misery of the world with the goodness of God. One psalm, though one only, ends in despair, Psalm 88. Another, Psalm 49, arrives at a position which seems adequately if perhaps unwittingly summarized by Professor Hocking: "A rude mechanical justice, operating without noise, incessantly reduces to common dust all the mounting conquests of personal prowess and distributes their yield to new hands."[30] "Man though in honor (or, like an ox) cannot abide, he is like the beasts that perish." Still another, Psalm 73, one of the most inspiring of all the collection, produces two solutions, of which the first, the impending doom of the ungodly, in William Temple's words, is "theoretical and false," for the wicked do not "perish and come to a fearful end." The Psalter is full of similar misstatements. This dogma of the psalmist, says the Archbishop, "is both false and even reprehensible. At a higher stage in the religious development of Israel the author

[30] "Positive Meanings of Death," in *Thoughts on Death and Life* (New York, 1937), p. 15.

of the Book of Job represents the Almighty Himself as pronouncing censure upon the three friends of Job for enunciating precisely this dogma."[31] But the other solution, the lesson of his own experience, his realization that having found God he has discovered the true riches, is "empirical and unassailable."

But I am always with thee,
> thou dost hold me by my right hand.
With thy counsel thou dost lead me,
> and take me in the path of glory.
Whom have I in heaven but thee
> and beside thee I have no delight on earth.
When my flesh and my mind fail,
> the Lord is my rock . . . and my portion forever.

"That," says Archbishop Temple, "is the real solution — not an answer to the riddle, but the attainment of a state of mind in which there is no desire to ask it."[32]

As this psalm illustrates, in the majority of cases in which trouble is mentioned, the *cause* of suffering or evil is not stated. "When I thought to know this, it was too painful (or troublesome) for me." The psalmist's usual response to the situation is not speculation but trust. Suffering, so far from destroying his belief in a good God, on the contrary confirms it.

This amazing ability of the Hebrew people to turn adversity into a more penetrating and firmer faith is nowhere better exemplified than in the psalms. Notice how many of the favorites express trust, 23, 121, 46, 103, 84, 91, 42–43, 27, 126 and 139, to give but a few examples. In the eight brief verses of Psalm 121, for instance, the root *to protect, guard, keep safe*, occurs six times. The very titles given to God in the psalms make the point: Rock, Fortress, Shield, Support, Light, Salvation, Hope, Confidence, Helper and Savior. And if one undertakes to list expressions of trust in

[31] *Nature, Man and God* (London, 1934), p. 42f. [32] *Ibid.*, p. 43.

THE PSALMS

the psalms his table may well include many of the noblest words of the Bible. These are but a few:

I will both lay me down in peace and sleep; for thou, Lord, only makest me dwell in safety. (4:8)

Yea, though I walk through the valley of the shadow of death, I will fear no evil, for thou art with me. (23:4)

The Lord is my light and my salvation; whom shall I fear? The Lord is the strength of my life; of whom shall I be afraid? (27:1)

Into thine hand I commit my spirit: thou hast redeemed me, O Lord God of truth. (31:5)

How excellent is thy loving kindness, O God! therefore the children of men put their trust under the shadow of thy wings. (36:7)

Why art thou cast down, O my soul, and why art thou disquieted within me? Hope thou in God: for I shall yet praise him, who is the health of my countenance, and my God. (42:11)

God is our refuge and our strength, a very present help in trouble. Therefore will not we fear . . . Be still, and know that I am God. The Lord of hosts is with us, the God of Jacob is our refuge. (46:1, 2, 10, 11)

In thee, O Lord, do I put my trust: let me never be put to confusion. (71:1 — and the *Te Deum*)

Whom have I in Heaven but thee? and there is none upon earth that I desire beside thee. My flesh and my heart faileth, but God is the strength of my heart, and my portion forever. (73:25f.)

For the Lord God is a sun and shield: the Lord will give grace and glory, no good thing will be withheld from them that walk uprightly. (84:11)

For he shall give his angels charge over thee, to keep thee in all thy ways. (91:11)

Like as a father pitieth his children, so the Lord pitieth them that fear him. (103:13)

He will not suffer thy foot to be moved: he that keepeth thee will not slumber. (121:3)

Let Israel hope in the Lord, for with the Lord there is mercy, and with him is plenteous redemption. (130:7)

And this passage taken from the psalm which Ibn Ezra in the twelfth century called "very glorious, in these five books there is none like it," and others "the crown of the Psalter."—

> Whither shall I go from thy spirit?
> Or whither shall I flee from thy presence?
> If I ascend up into heaven, thou art there:
> If I make my bed in Sheol, behold, thou art there.
> If I take the wings of the morning,
> And dwell in the uttermost parts of the sea;
> Even there shall thy hand lead me,
> And thy right hand shall hold me.
>
> (139:7 ff.)

The ground of trust, as can be seen from the above, is God's love, his "mercy" or "loving-kindness," more accurately his "affectionate loyalty" or "friendship" (ḥesed), a word which appears one hundred and twenty-seven times in the psalms. It is this which was from everlasting and endures forever. What happens to man after his death is not stated, but the awareness of God's love now gives assurance for any future in this life or another. This religion does not defer its dividends. It does not compensate for a black present by promises of a bright but remote future. It does not hold out immortality for all who are initiated into "the happy mystic bands." [33] But beside the deep faith of the psalms, the shallow assertion that life goes on or that the dead are resuscitated, regardless of morals or the development of the spirit this side of the grave, is "faith in knickerbockers." "To believe," says George Tyrrell, "that this terrible machine-world is really from God, in God and unto God, that through it and in spite of its blind fatality all works together for good, that is faith in long trousers." [34] The psalmists, although they did not believe in a machine

---

[33] Aristophanes *Frogs* 454.
[34] Cf. M. D. Petre (ed.), *George Tyrrell's Letters* (London, 1920), p. 151.

world, likewise had a mature, long-trousered faith: that God rules, that there are no limits to his love, and that man has dignity and majesty through his capacity for fellowship in mind and spirit with his Creator.

When I behold . . . the work of thy fingers, the moon and the
    stars which thou hast ordained,
What is man, that thou shouldest remember him, or the son
    of man, that thou shouldest notice him? [35]

In a word, the power of the psalms may be that they tell the truth about God, to whom belong the world and its fulness, and the truth about man, shapen in iniquity, never to be confused with his holy Creator, whom God made nevertheless little less than *Elohim*, not angels only, but deity, divinity, Himself.

[35] Ps. 8:3f.

A TWICE-BURIED APOCALYPSE

CHARLES CUTLER TORREY
Yale University

The title sounds sensational, but it will be found to be fully justified. The "buried" book is the Apocalypse of the Hebrew prince Shealtiel the father of Zerubbabel. It was buried the first time because of its conspicuously false prediction, and was at once supplanted by the so-called Apocalypse of Baruch, which made free use of its material. Fifteen or twenty years later it was resurrected again, this time to be incorporated in an "Apocalypse of Ezra," the Second Esdras of the Apocrypha of our English Bible.

The fortunes and misfortunes of this book in its successive transformations constitute one of the most interesting and instructive episodes in all the history of the Jewish apocalypses. The theory presented here is essentially new, though incidental features of it have appeared elsewhere, as will be shown.

Our Second Esdras (known to European scholars as Fourth Ezra) is well known to be a composite book, in fact it is doubly composite. In the first place, it has a false head and a false tail. Chapters 1, 2, 15, and 16 do not belong to the main body of the book, but were added to it in the Roman west; the oriental versions do not contain these chapters at all. Again, this work which now masquerades as the "Apocalypse of Ezra" had originally nothing to do with Ezra. As may be seen in the very first verse (3:1), it consisted of the visions of Shealtiel [1] the father of Zerub-

---

[1] The Greek translation, from which all the known versions of the book are derived, employed the LXX form of the name, Salathiel. Since, however, we now know the original language of the book to have been Semitic (in fact, it was Aramaic), the Semitic form of the name is to be preferred.

babel, and it included chapters 3–13 of the present book, entire and very nearly in the form which we now see. It was eventually taken over for Ezra by inserting his name five times, making numerous slight alterations in chapters 11 and 12 (namely, in the vision which provides the *date* of the book), and by affixing an Ezra legend, chapter 14, at the end.

The whole work, Second Esdras, has been a favorite from the first, and very influential. Its great reputation comes from the inner document, the Shealtiel revelation, which is a noble specimen of Jewish theology of the first century A.D., lost to sight, however, in its true character until now.

It is necessary to establish at the outset the relation between the Apocalypse of Shealtiel (in the sequel represented by the letter S) and another document which resembles it very closely and is intimately connected with its history. This is the Apocalypse of Baruch (in the sequel represented by the letter B), a less familiar work, but one which also has been widely influential.[2] It seems to come from the same time, and out of the same conditions, as the visions of Shealtiel. It has the same subject and treats it in much the same way. The resemblance is so close as to constitute a famous literary problem, which has not hitherto been satisfactorily solved. Just what is the relation between the two books? The following parallels, a few selected from many, may serve to show in how significant a way the one document duplicates the other.

The seer Shealtiel, head of the Jewish exiles in Babylonia (see 5:16f.), is in distress over the destruction of Jerusalem and the temple by Nebuchadrezzar, and cannot see how

---

[2] Several Baruch apocalypses are known to us. The one here taken into account is sometimes called the Syriac Apocalypse of Baruch, since it is only in that language that it is preserved entire. In Charles's *Apocrypha*, II, 470 ff., it is entitled II Baruch.

God could have allowed this to happen. Are the Babylonians better than the Israelites? Have they been more attentive to the divine commandments? An angel is sent to instruct him, and he debates, through the angel, with the Most High. There are successive visions, interrupted by seven-day periods of fasting.

The seer Baruch the son of Neriah, the secretary and companion of the prophet Jeremiah, has a revelation just before the arrival of Nebuchadrezzar's army, to the effect that Jerusalem and the temple are to be destroyed. He is in deep distress; why is Babylon prospered and Zion desolate? Who then shall speak the praises of the Lord or know the divine law? In a series of visions he holds long dialogues with the Most High. (Instruction by the angel is reserved for a special section.) The visions are interrupted by fasts of seven days each. The general plan of the one book is thus like that of the other.

Whoever compares the two apocalypses is constantly coming across striking phrases which are found in both works; Charles in his *Apocalypse of Baruch* (1896), pp. 170 f., has collected sixty-six examples of such verbal parallels. The following are chosen at random.

If God delivers his people into the hands of ungodly nations, "what will he then do for his Name by which we are called?" S 4:25 = B 5:1, end.

Where the seer is addressed, the righteous Israelites are often referred to by the phrase "those who are like you" (or, like Abraham, or some other saint); thus, S 4:36; 8:51, 62; 14:9,49; B 13:5; 21:24; 57:1; 59:1; 66:7. The phrase is noticeable, even aside from the frequent repetition.

Moses "brought the law to the seed of Jacob, and the commandment to the nation of Israel." S 3:19 = B 17:4.

In the last great day God will especially protect "those who are found in this land." S 13:48f. = B 29:2.

There are "store-chambers containing the souls of the

righteous," and these are guarded by angels. See S 4:35, 41; 7:32, 80, 95; B 21:23; 24:1; 30:2.

There is more conspicuous duplication, thus, an entire scene. The seer, whether Baruch or Shealtiel, wishes to go away by himself, for fasting and meditation. Baruch says (32:7): "Draw not near me for a few days, nor seek me, till I come to you." Shealtiel says (5:19): "Come not nigh me for seven days, and then shalt thou come to me."

Baruch's companions reply: "Why dost thou forsake us, as a father who forsakes his orphan children? If thou forsakest us, it were better for us all to die before thee." Shealtiel's companion says: "Forsake us not, as a shepherd that leaveth his flock among cruel wolves. If thou forsakest us, it had been better for us if we had been consumed in the burning of Zion" (12:44).

Baruch says: "Far be it from me to forsake you; I go to enquire concerning you and Zion." Shealtiel says: "I have not forsaken you; I am come to pray for the desolation of Zion."

The following example is very striking. Both books give much attention to Adam's fall and the doctrine of original sin. In both books there is a cry of dismay addressed to our sinning ancestor. Shealtiel cries (7:118), "O Adam, what hast thou done? for though it was thou that sinned, the evil is not fallen on thee alone, but upon all of us that come of thee!" In Baruch we read (48:42), "O Adam, what hast thou done to all those that are born from thee?"

Such a dramatic apostrophe as this is doubly conspicuous, too much so for any ordinary case of borrowing. It is no wonder that some scholars have held the opinion that both books came from the same author. This, however, is an impossible supposition, for the two authors differ markedly in temperament and outlook, as all recent commentators agree. What we see is undisguised appropriation on a large scale, the later author feeling free to make use of the material of his predecessor.

The question of priority is insistent, and much depends on its answer, as will appear. Most students of the two books now hold that "Second Esdras" is the older, arguing from its profound philosophy and its literary quality. There are advocates of the contrary view, however, and Schürer, *Geschichte*, III, 227, declares the question still open. I think that it can be finally settled.

Many have seen in B 54:15–19, "Each one of us has been the Adam of his own soul," a mitigation of S 3:21f., 7:118ff., "Adam transgressed, and so must all those who are born of him." Schürer's attempt (*ibid.*) to refute this opinion is not convincing.

There is still clearer evidence. The passage B 29:4 concerning Behemoth and Leviathan is taken directly from 2 Esd. 6:49–52. Not only is the diction verbally the same throughout the passage, but in the case of each of the two monsters there is plain allusion to details given only in S. R. H. Charles, *Apocalypse of Baruch*, p. 53, sets this forth clearly, saying that "so far, 4 Ezra would seem to be the source of our text." Yet because of his dating of the two books (he regards B as the older) he is unable to accept this natural explanation, but must postulate a third document from which both B and S derive their material!

I would call attention, further, to a very curious passage which in B immediately precedes the mention of Behemoth and Leviathan. It relates to the "consummation of the times" (27:15), the last act in which the nations of the earth take part. The verse 28:2 reads: "For the measure and reckoning of that time are two parts weeks of seven weeks" (*duae partes hebdomades septem hebdomadarum*). This is nonsense, and no one has succeeded in making sense from it. We are familiar with the apocalyptic "week" of seven *years*, and it will be seen that in the present passage the Latin translator should have written *annorum*.

The problematic "two parts" finds its explanation in 2 Esd. 7:28-44. At the close of the 400 years of the Messiah son of Joseph (*nota bene!*) all life on earth will cease. Thereupon will follow two periods of seven "days" each; first a period of rest (vss. 30 f.), then a period of judgment (vss. 33-44), and of the latter is said that "it shall endure as it were a week of years." Here, evidently, are the two measures of time referred to in the single verse B 28:2, where (as already said) the true reading must be "two parts, weeks of seven *years*." The priority of S, in any case, is certain.

Charles, who holds fast to the contrary view, and in his *Pseudepigrapha* puts "Second Baruch" before "Fourth Ezra," has some seemingly firm ground for his opinion. He regards B (he would say, the older part of B), with good reason, as antedating the capture of Jerusalem by Titus; see below. In the dating of Second Esdras he is in agreement with the almost universally accepted verdict, demanded by the present text of the book, that it was composed in the time of Domitian. I shall attempt to show in the following pages that this view is mistaken. The Ezra Apocalypse, indeed, was published in the time of Domitian, but this is merely a later and garbled expansion of the Shealtiel Apocalypse.

Here, now, is a puzzling problem. Why did the later writer, B, borrow from S in this very conspicuous manner, as though he could be confident that the fact of his plagiarism would be unknown to the public? Also, why did he borrow at all? for the author of the Apocalypse of Baruch was a man of originality and lively imagination, one who had a theology of his own; his book is full of interesting matter not found in Second Esdras. He had no need to borrow from anyone. Was his book composed in some haste,

A TWICE-BURIED APOCALYPSE

perhaps designed to meet the same crisis which had faced his predecessor?

The rescue of Israel was to be brought about by the advent of a Messiah, and this was uniformly prophesied to take place in a time of foreign oppression and general uproar, a time when Israel would be in dire distress and threatened with catastrophe (Is. 17:12–14; Zech. 14:1–4, etc.). Every such time was likely to bring forth its apocalypse.

There was one time in Jewish history when the stage was set for the coming of the Deliverer more clearly, perhaps, than at any other time. This was in the chaos which followed the death of Nero, chaos which in the west amounted to civil war, while in the east to both Jews and Christians it seemed plainly to mean the end of the present age. No other emperor had made so deep a personal impression as Nero, not only in Rome but throughout the Roman world. More than this, he was the last member of the Julian house, of the legitimate line whose members had been permitted to rule the world. He himself was the sixth emperor in the series, counting Julius Caesar; on this reckoning, see below. The apparent dissolution of the great empire after Nero's reign brought forth more than one prophecy of the approaching end of the present age. The New Testament book of Revelation, written in the year 68 (Torrey, *Documents of the Primitive Church*, pp. 242–244), foresaw *seven* completed reigns (the sacred number), and the great catastrophe coming in the eighth reign, that of Nero *redivivus*. Now comes another, very similar prediction.

The all-important question is that of the date of the earlier work, the Apocalypse of Shealtiel, which (as was said above) begins at chapter 3 of our Second Esdras and continues to the end of chapter 13. Its author dated it for us; but, as we shall see, his date has been purposely disguised by a later hand to such an extent that what was simple has become a labyrinth. Fortunately, the original date can still be discovered.

Apocalypses are frequently dated by means of a symbolic picture of some sort. Successive scenes or details stand for successive periods of time, coming at last to the writer's own day; and then, if we have any luck, we may see when it was that he wrote. Daniel's four strange beasts represented four successive world-empires. In the book of Revelation, the seven heads of the monster (chapter 17) stood for seven Roman emperors. In Enoch, there is a procession of sheep and rams that comes to a stop in the middle of the Hasmonean period.

In our Second Esdras there is a famous example of the kind, the "vision of the eagle," which has given rise to much literature. The vision itself is described in chapter 11 and the first nine verses of chapter 12; the interpretation, given by the angel, follows in 12:10–34. Shealtiel has a dream, in which he sees an eagle coming up out of the sea. The interpretation, furnished by the angel Uriel, declares the eagle to represent the Roman empire, and her wings to represent certain "kings."

According to the evidence which will presently be given, the vision originally continued in this way: "I saw, and behold, she spread her wings over all the earth, and all the winds of heaven blew on her, and the clouds were gathered together about her. And as I looked, the eagle flew with her wings, to reign over the earth and over them that dwell therein. And I beheld how all things under heaven were subject to her, and no man spoke against her, no, not one creature upon earth. And I numbered her wings, and behold, there were eight of them."

This would seem to make the matter rather simple, in view of our knowledge of Roman history. The only uncertainty would be in the question whether the author of the book began his series of Roman emperors with Julius Caesar or with Augustus. Both modes of reckoning were in use. In the New Testament book of Revelation the series is made to begin with Augustus, as is made quite plain; here, also, the question is answered at once, very clearly. Soon after the verse (11) which tells of the eight wings, an announcement is made to the second emperor in the great series, at the time of his death: "There shall none after thee attain unto thy time, nor even unto the half thereof." The second "wing," then, was Augustus, who reigned more than fifty years; not even Tiberius reigned the half of this time. The first wing was Julius Caesar.

Before we can think of dating the vision, however, there is much to be done, for the original text, as was remarked above, has been deliberately altered. In particular, the scheme of *seven* has now been replaced by the other sacred number, *twelve*, and over the picture drawn by the first writer is now spread a network of curious details evidently intended to be mystifying. The eagle which came up out of the sea had now "twelve feathered wings and three heads" (and the heads are declared to represent Roman emperors); also, "out of her wings there grew other wings over against them, and they became little wings." When the "eight wings" of verse 11 are mentioned, they are declared to be the little wings (or, some of the little wings?) that were "over against" the others; and in the interpretation (12:20) they are said to represent "kings" whose reigns were short (*how* short?). The climax of the calculated mystification is reached in 11:21, where it is said that "some of" the wings (how many??) did not reign at all!

Even without this, there had been uncertainty enough. Does the later apocalyptist make his vision of the eagle cover the reigns of twelve emperors? or twenty? or twenty-three? or some number between these limits? In fact, some modern interpreters of the vision have carried it down as far as the reigns of Caracalla and Macrinus (early third century). Not only these interpreters but many others, including G. H. Box in Charles's *Pseudepigrapha*, pronounce the eagle vision an interpolation, not belonging to this apocalypse!

There is, nevertheless, a rather definite and highly important date given, in the midst of all this confusion. Nearly all recent commentators agree that the "three heads" of the eagle are the three Flavian emperors, Vespasian, Titus, and Domitian, and accordingly, that the apocalypse of Ezra must have been put forth at some time in Domitian's reign. Evidence in support of these conclusions is to be seen in the verses 12:14, 16, 18, 23ff.; notice especially the thrice-repeated "twelve," the sacred number. The author of the expanded work thought that he saw the plan of the Almighty for the line of Caesars; after the twelfth had been permitted to finish his reign the End would come! He may have been as fully convinced of this as his predecessor, or the author of the book of Revelation, had been of the finality of the number seven, nevertheless he wrote obscurely, to leave the mystery open; his predecessor had made the fatal mistake of a false prediction. Still another "hedge" is seen in the astonishing date(!) which he gives in 14:48 (not in the Latin text nor in the English Apocrypha).

The way is now open for seeking, in the vision of the eagle, the date of the original writing, the Apocalypse of Shealtiel. In the verses 11:36f. the vision has come down to the author's own day. Now appears the roaring lion symbolizing the Messiah son of Joseph, [3] whose advent

[3] See above, and cf. 7:28f. with 13:1ff. The words which the Syriac version inserts in 12:32 are a false interpretation. The Ephraimite Messiah dies at the end of his long career (which seems to be described in the Baruch Apocalypse, chapter 29); the Jewish tradition knows of no death of the Davidic Messiah.

A TWICE-BURIED APOCALYPSE

follows close upon certain events which are given a definite description. If these events can be located with certainty, we have the date of this apocalypse.

Verses 32–35 tell of one great ruler, who is succeeded by two of less importance who are deadly rivals, the one eventually compassing the death of the other. Of the great ruler is said, that he "held the whole earth in possession and ruled over those that dwell therein with much oppression; and he had the governance of the world more than all the wings that had been." Of a sudden, he appeared no more (vs. 33). Of the two wings that then followed, the one "devoured" the other.

There is only one Roman emperor to whom the description of this "great ruler" could possibly apply, and that is the emperor Nero. It suits his reign perfectly. After his "sudden" end (see the interpretation, below), the two rivals that followed were Galba and Otho, the former slain by the latter. Thereupon the roar of the lion is heard.

Was this apocalypse (or, *an* apocalypse) written in the time of Otho, 69 A.D.? It is not likely that any interpreter, of the great number who have discussed the vision, has ever suggested this date. It has appeared to be ruled out at once by the enumeration of *twelve* (or, twenty?) emperors plus "three heads." The fact has not been seen that the eagle vision was revised ingeniously and thoroughly with the express aim of hiding from sight the original dating.

It may be added here, that there is in the passage 11:38–46 good evidence that the vision was composed before the advent of Titus in Jerusalem. Verses 40–42 contain the detailed accusation brought by the Most High against the Roman empire. It is all set forth in the most general terms, the peoples of the earth have been treated cruelly and unjustly by Daniel's "fourth beast," but there is no indication that the Most High is concerned with anything that the Romans have brought upon his chosen people and his holy city. The argument from silence is sometimes very powerful, and this is an instance.

There is one point at which alteration of the original text can be seen with especial clearness, the point where alteration *must* be made, in the passage which gave ground for the original dating. Parallel columns can best show how the details of the vision itself in chapter 11 are made over and rendered incomprehensible by garbling the interpretation given by the angel in chapter 12.

11:32–35	12:23–28
This **head** held the whole earth in possession, and bore rule over those that dwell therein, with much oppression; and it had the governance of the world more than all the wings that had been.	In the last days shall the Most High raise up **three kings** . . . and **they** shall bear rule over the earth and over those that dwell therein, with much oppression, above all those that were before **them**. . . .
And after this I beheld, and lo, this **head** suddenly appeared no more.	And whereas thou sawest that the great **head** appeared no more, it signifieth that **one of them** shall die on his bed, and yet with pain.
But there remained two **heads**, which also in like sort reigned over the earth and over those that dwell therein.	But for the two that remained, the sword shall devour them.
And I beheld, and lo, the **head** upon the right side devoured it that was upon the left side.	For the sword of the one shall devour him that was with him; but he also shall fall by the sword in the last days.

The attempt to make the picture of Nero fit the three Flavian emperors(!) is quite futile. Nor can any acceptable sense be made out of the statements regarding the "three heads" and their relations, in the new setting. Words which in the Apocalypse of Shealtiel had expressed simple historical fact have become mere nonsense in this later application. A minor aid to the obfuscation is seen in the substitution of the word "head" for "wing."

A most interesting and valuable hint is given in 12:26. It

was said in the vision that the great wing (Nero) "suddenly appeared no more" (11:33). This is given a curiously worded interpretation in the next chapter: "Whereas thou sawest that the great head appeared no more, it signifieth that 'one of them' (!!) shall die upon his bed, and yet with pain." This is a plain allusion to the tragic death of Nero, who committed suicide, with a short sword, on his own bed.[4] Of the two successors, Galba and Otho, "the sword of the one devoured his fellow."

It is not mere coincidence that Otho is *the eighth* Roman emperor in this series. We may now turn back to the verse 11:11 and read, with new assurance, "I numbered the wings, and behold, there were eight of them."

It is easy to see why the vision of the eagle had to be revised, if it continued to be used. Its prediction (which proved false) was too evident, unmistakable. False prophecies, in the Jewish and Christian scriptures, are hardly rare, but it is almost always possible to explain them away. Daniel's prophecy of the death of Antiochus as the closing event of the present age has generally been interpreted out of sight. The unusually plain predictions made by the author of the book of Revelation are at present explained away by practically all scholars. The prediction in Mark's Gospel, combining the statue and purpose of Caligula with the exactly similar statue and purpose of Antiochus set forth in the book of Daniel, is generally unrecognized. The apostle Paul gave the Thessalonians a promise on divine authority, an actual "word" (which he found in the 13th chapter of Mark), that the second coming of Christ would be in their generation. This is variously discounted.

The prediction made in Shealtiel's vision of the eagle, on the contrary, could not be explained away. The allusion

---

[4] It is obvious that the reviser understood perfectly the allusion, and was unwilling to transfer the suicide to any other emperor, hence his "one of them."

to Nero and his two rival successors was unmistakable, and the symbolism of the eight wings made the certainty more certain. The angel of revelation, fresh from heaven, is declared to have told the Hebrew prince that the Messiah would come in the time of Otho. The Messiah did *not* come; therefore, necessarily, these visions of Shealtiel were discredited and discarded.

The prophecy was too important a thing, however, to be thrown away and lost. It was recognized as one of the finest products of the theology of its time, and its value for the instruction of the Jewish people was evident, especially in this time when the fourth and last beast of Daniel's great prophecy was in the throes of death.

Here, I think, is where the Apocalypse of Baruch comes in. Some one made a free use of the material of the discredited book, including its framework, some definite scenes, and much of its phraseology; yet producing a very different work containing a large amount of new and interesting material. This time, there was no attempt at definite prediction of the day of deliverance, though the author, writing under the name of Baruch, was as certain as his predecessor had been that the advent of the Messiah was immediately at hand.

Whoever will read carefully chapters 68–70 will see that in this miniature of Jewish history from the exile to the advent of the Messiah there is nothing to indicate that the author had knowledge of the catastrophe of 70 A.D. Indeed, the only passage in the whole intensely patriotic work where such allusion is made is in the three verses 32:2–4, which are bracketed by Charles as a later insertion. They are indicated as such not only for the good reasons which Charles gives, but also because it is really inconceivable that the author of the book could have been content with this one obscure and colorless allusion.[5]

[5] The reason why the insertion was made is easy to see: the reference

A TWICE-BURIED APOCALYPSE

The Apocalypse of Baruch, then, was composed at some time in the year 69. It was intended by its author to supplant the Apocalypse of Shealtiel, which had very recently appeared and was now rendered useless by its false prediction. Much of the material of the eclipsed and abandoned work was incorporated (as shown above) in the new publication. The few existing copies of the Apocalypse of Shealtiel were allowed to perish; this was its *first* "burial." One copy at least was preserved, however, as will appear.

To return now to the eagle vision, and the curious alteration of the original text: mention was made above of the emphasis on the number twelve. It appears in the first verse and is repeated in 11:22, and then in 12:14 we read: "In [this kingdom] shall twelve kings reign, one after another, and the second shall have a longer reign than any other of the twelve. This is the interpretation of the twelve wings which thou sawest." Apparently, the author of the second edition, seeing that the Most High had passed over the sacred number seven in this case, had no doubt that he had preferred to use the sacred number twelve.

Due notice is taken of the chaos which followed the death of Nero, 12:18: "In the midst of the time of that kingdom ... it shall stand in peril of falling; nevertheless it shall not then fall, but shall be restored again to its first estate." The eagle had been a sick bird, but has recovered and taken on weight. It is clearly the belief of this writer, however, that the End is now at hand (12:23): "In the last days the Most High will raise up three kings.... They are called the heads of the eagle because they are those that shall finish her last end." Domitian was the twelfth emperor in this series and the last of the three "heads," as modern commentators very generally agree.

---

to Haggai 2:6 in vs. 1 naturally suggested to a reader the next following verses of the prophecy, especially vs. 9, and the temptation to let Baruch foretell the destruction by the Romans was too strong to be resisted.

The history of the new book, now contained in our "Second Esdras," is easily traced. A copy of the Apocalypse of Shealtiel had been preserved. No one could read it without being deeply impressed; it probably was felt to be divinely inspired scripture, in spite of the (unauthorized) prediction in the figure of the eagle. However this may be, the precious document was saved and made useful by means of a new literary framework, given a *third* lease of life by attaching it to the great name of Ezra the Scribe. This was done in the most economical manner possible, by making a few slight interpolations and appending a single chapter giving the account (in the first person) of Ezra's restoration of the entire Old Testament, which had been destroyed when the Chaldeans took Jerusalem.

The following interpolations are especially to be noted.

In the first verse of the first chapter of the newly constituted Apocalypse of Ezra (2 Esd. 3:1) we read: "I, Shealtiel (that is, Ezra),[6] was in Babylon," etc. In like manner the name "Esdras" (vocative case) is simply inserted in 6:10; 7:1, 25; and 8:2.

At the point where the Ezra chapter (chap. 14) is appended to the Shealtiel book a little patch is necessary, to keep the transition from being too abrupt. The limits of this patch are very obvious, and it has been marked off by more than one scholar independently. It consists of the verses 53b–56 and the last clause of verse 57.[7]

---

[6] Why (it is natural to ask) was not the name "Shealtiel" simply *omitted* in the revision? The answer is, that the Hebrew scribes avoided on principle omitting anything that had been written, in their religious literature. They could contradict it, or add to it, or (in some cases) replace it by a true equivalent, but to remove it altogether they recognized no right.

[7] This redactional insertion and also the interpolations of the name Esdras are recognized by G. H. Box in *The Ezra Apocalypse* (1912) and in his treatment of the book in Charles's *Pseudepigrapha*, though he has a very different and complicated theory of the composition of the book, generally following Kabisch, *Das vierte Buch Esra* (1889).

The man who composed and added the 14th chapter, and who made the interpolations just described, was also the one who made over the vision of the eagle into its present astonishing form. His purpose in the last-named case was chiefly to produce obscurity, no doubt, but also to make a cautiously veiled prediction of the speedy coming of the Messiah. Some details of his confusing scheme of "wings" and "heads" may perhaps be plausibly interpreted, though no important result can be gained. He certainly wrote in the time of Domitian.

The attempt to disguise and rename the resurrected prophecy of Shealtiel — burying it for the second time — was completely successful. The entire work is known and studied at the present day as "The Apocalypse of Ezra."

SUPERFLUOUS καί IN THE LORD'S PRAYER AND ELSEWHERE

HENRY JOEL CADBURY
Harvard University

Considering its brevity, its simplicity and its importance the Lord's Prayer provides an extraordinary number of difficulties to anyone who would quote it in English. Even if for convenience of congregational recitation one is content to retain arbitrarily older English renderings, there is still the fact that Luke's form is different from Matthew's even in the King James Version, and the further inconvenience that Matthew's form, if that is preferred as the fuller and more liturgical, is current in two well established forms, one with "debts" and "debtors" in the King James text, and the other with "trespasses" and "them that trespass against us" in the Book of Common Prayer.[1]

The conscientious scholar will of course reckon with other difficulties. Primary among these is the fact that one word, ἐπιούσιος, though it occurs in both gospels and hence probably comes from their common Greek source, is to all intents and purposes without parallel in other context. The single occurrence finally discovered in a Greek papyrus (Preisigke, *Sammelbuch*, i. 5224) is only a tantalization to us and does not prevent us from admitting that whether the word means daily or not we really do not know. Another ambiguity has to do with the gender of "the evil." One of the most criticized changes of the revisers of 1881 was the choice of the masculine implied in their rendering "and deliver us from the evil *one*." But it is a thoroughly

[1] It is not only more widely used but is older than the form of the Authorized Version, being found in the first edition of Tyndal, in the primers of 1538 and 1545, and in the prayerbook since 1549. The King James form was anticipated by all the Bible versions except Tyndal. See J. W. Thirtle, *The Lord's Prayer* (1915) pp. 214-217.

justified alternative, and still leaves open the question whether it means the devil, or whether it means humanly and generically the evil man.[2]

The textual variants in the passages are few, but they further embarrass the translator. The doxology certainly does not belong in Matthew any more than in Luke. It is pretty clear that "forgave" (past) is more probably what first stood in Matthew than "forgive" (present). Here again is another pitfall since even such good scholars as Wellhausen and Harnack have called ἀφήκαμεν a perfect, not recognizing its aorist form. Luke's prayer which so many MSS have assimilated in many places to Matthew's form seems very likely to have had as its second petition not "may thy kingdom come" but "may thy Holy Spirit come upon us and cleanse us."

This familiar and yet challenging passage may be a suitable text for raising a small question of translation about the commonest of all Greek words, καί. Both gospels use it here, but somewhat differently, in connection with our forgiving of others.

Matt.: ὡς καὶ ἡμεῖς ἀφήκαμεν τοῖς ὀφειλέταις ἡμῶν
Luke: καὶ γὰρ αὐτοὶ ἀφίομεν παντὶ ὀφείλοντι ἡμῖν

In such contexts it is usual and unobjectionable to translate literally with an "even" or an "also." Does such treatment

[2] A similar ambiguity in the substantive use of the same adjective occurs a few verses earlier (Mt. 6:38) in the injunction not to resist the evil (τῷ πονηρῷ). Here the devil at least is excluded, since resisting the devil is regarded as praiseworthy. Modern recognition of the place held in Jewish thought by the evil impulse, yeṣer ha-raʻ, makes the modern translator less sure than the revisers of 1881 that he should translate the Lord's Prayer, "deliver us from the evil one." In fact, the closest parallel to the whole passage is in Bab. Berakot 60b, where deliverance from the evil impulse is sought. For further examples see F. C. Porter, "The Yeçer Hara," in *Biblical and Semitic Studies ... of Yale University* (1902) p. 130.

really represent best in English the whole feeling in Greek of such passages, especially in the Matthean version, or were the translators of the King James Version better advised in leaving it out altogether?[3]

As for Luke's clause, the exact meaning of καὶ γάρ in New Testament usage is disputable and in fact it may be various. The καί, if not completely superfluous, may as in classical Greek with difficulty be translated, since it adds the reason given by καί as a new consideration to the preceding sentence, rather than emphasizing any word in the γάρ clause. In Luke αὐτοί already emphasizes "we" that forgive as does only in slightly less degree the expressed pronoun ἡμεῖς in Matthew. Of the other instances in Luke-Acts of καὶ γάρ (Lk. 1:66; 6:32; 7:8; 21: 37 v.l.; 21:59; Acts 19:40) some at least invite reminiscence of the classical idiom, where "for . . . also" is hardly the right rendering.[4]

In relative clauses, however, whether introduced by a pronoun, or as in Matthew's form of the Lord's Prayer by an adverb, the superfluous character of the καί is more evident, and I think the translator of the New Testament is well advised often to leave out any English equivalent.[5]

The intrusion of such words in the history of language is easily understood. The relative pronoun is in Greek a simple monosyllable, easily confused in sound and writing with other words and naturally attracting support. I think I have established elsewhere the probability that in Hellenistic Greek such support was found for the nominative forms of the relative pronoun, ἥ, οἵ, αἵ by frequent substitutions of ἥτις, οἵτινες, αἵτινες.[6] Among other forms of

---

[3] In Matthew "even as we" is the reading of Tyndal and the Geneva Bible; "as we also" of Coverdale, Rheims and Revised Version; "as we" of the Great Bible, the Bishops' Bible, and the Authorized Version.

[4] Cf. F. W. Grosheide, "καὶ γάρ in het N. T.," *Theologische Studien*, 33 (1915) 108–110.

[5] This has often been done in the Revised Standard Version.

[6] *Journal of Biblical Literature* 42 (1923), 150–157.

strengthening relative pronouns I mentioned there some Biblical instances where καί seems to be used in much the same way to bolster the weak relative and suggested "a further study of this colorless use of καί in relative clauses (which appears also in the papyri)." The present is a brief contribution to that study.

The confirmation of this feeling, (and in such matters one depends on linguistic sense and wide reading more than on proof) I can only indicate. Concordances to Hellenistic writings are not so arranged as to make easy any complete statistical data concerning such common words as καί and the relatives. Besides, in every such case a literal rendering with "also" is always possible. Our question is rather whether it does not usually over-translate the original. Here are two English examples of the neuter relative pronoun from Luke-Acts:

> Acts 11:29f. And the disciples. . . . determined to send relief unto the brethren that dwelt in Judaea, which also they did (ὃ καὶ ἐποίησαν), sending, etc.
>
> Acts 26:9f. I verily thought with myself that I ought to do many things contrary to the name of Jesus of Nazareth. And this I also did (ὃ καὶ ἐποίησα) in Jerusalem.

We recall that the likeness of the former of these to Galatians 2:10, "only they would that we should remember the poor; which very thing I was also zealous to do" (ὃ καὶ ἐσπούδασα αὐτὸ τοῦτο ποιῆσαι) is one of the very few linguistic grounds for supposing that the author of Acts had read Paul's letters. Even if the occasion is the same, the only real likeness is the identical ὃ καί which with such a common verb as ποιέω might easily be independent. The combination εἰς ὃ καί occurs in 2 Thess. 1:11; Col. 1:29 and in 1 Peter 2:8.

A thinly disguised form of this same neuter singular relative is in the words formed by joining it to a preposition, καθό, παρό, and especially διό, and the tendency to follow these with καί is even more general and marked. While in Luke the cases are not especially frequent, in some writers they are much more so. The cases with and without καί may be compared thus:

	διό with καί	διό without καί
Luke-Acts	3	7
Paul	6	19
Justin, *Dialogue with Trypho*	8(9)	3
Athenagoras	4	1(2)

Blass-Debrunner § 451.5 in commenting on this διὸ καί notes that it is a favorite combination in Aristotle's *Athenian Constitution*. The same might be said of Diodorus Siculus (whose alternative is not διό without καί but διόπερ) and of many other writers. διὸ καί is very common in the papyri, even in the Ptolemaic period as Mayser, *Grammatik*, II.3. p. 135 testifies.

Other instances of the relative pronoun with καί in Luke-Acts, but not in the neuter, include Luke 6:13f. ... he called the disciples; and he chose from them twelve whom also he named apostles (οὓς καὶ ἀποστόλους ὠνόμασεν): Simon, whom he also named Peter (ὃν καὶ ὠνόμασεν Πέτρον), etc.; 10:30; 10:39; Acts 1:2 ... after that he had given commandment through the Holy Spirit unto the apostles whom he had chosen, to whom he also showed himself alive (οἷς καὶ παρέστησεν ἑαυτὸν ζῶντα); 7:45; 10:39; 12:4; 13:22; 17:34; 28:10. Of course these constitute only a small fraction of the places where this author uses the relative pronoun and in each case an additional fact is implied so that a demonstrative pronoun with "and" could be used in translation (as is done in Acts 26:10 above). But the cases cited and those like them in other Greek writings of the period seem to me hardly classical. The καί is almost like the strengthening -περ.

I suppose ὡς may be regarded as the adverb of ὅς. Use with it of a superfluous καί is certainly common in Hellenistic Greek, and since a καί often occurs in the main clause associated with a comparison we now get καί in both clauses as at Mt. 18:33; Rom. 1:13. Of the καί with the comparative adverb the New Testament alone provides plenty of examples. In Acts ὡς καὶ ἡμεῖς (10:47), ὥσπερ καὶ ἐφ' ἡμᾶς (11:15), ὡς καὶ ἡμῖν (11:17), καθὼς καὶ ἡμῖν (15:18), follow in rapid succession and refer to the same circumstances. Other cases of ὡς καί in Acts are 13:33; 17:28; 22:5; 25:10. 2 Peter uses ὡς καί or καθὼς καί five times; 1 Thess. has καθὼς καί or καθάπερ καί nine times (without καί eight times). All these occur elsewhere in the New Testament, but καθώσπερ καί is limited to Hebrews 5:4.

Even when the Greek adverb of comparison was further elaborated into the full phrase καθ' ὃν τρόπον, which Justin Martyr regularly uses for an adverbial clause of comparison so that it becomes a trick of style,[7] the καί is frequently present, in Justin's *Apology* as i. 14, 1; 23, 3; 26, 6.

Not every occurrence of καί in such clauses is necessarily to be regarded as otiose. It is noticeable that the clause of comparison is more likely to include the καί when it follows the main clause. Perhaps this is because, as in our idiom, "also" is more appropriate and intelligible when that with which equation is made has been already mentioned. Conversely, when the subordinate clause of comparison precedes, the "also" seems to us more appropriate for the same reason in what is grammatically the main clause.[8] This is perhaps also to be found illustrated in Matthew's version of the Lord's Prayer where we read literally "as in

[7] B. L. Gildersleeve, *The Apologies of Justin Martyr* (1877) p. 114.
[8] E.g. Mt. 24:33 = Mk. 13:29 = Lk. 21:31.

heaven, also upon earth," ὡς ἐν οὐρανῷ καὶ ἐπὶ γῆς. Even the meticulous Revised Version had to paraphrase this to the extent of reading "so" here for "also."

Anyone familiar with the difference of feel between two languages will grant that any independent English writer would be less frequent in using the idioms here illustrated than the New Testament writers and men of near their time appear to have been. Our own little "as" is more commonly strengthened in another way, by prefixing "just."

Two analogies to these uses may be cited. (1) One is the use of καί to strengthen the prepositions meaning "with" (μετά and σύν). In our literature we have μετὰ καὶ Κλήμεντος (Phil. 4:3), σὺν καὶ Φορτυνάτῳ (1 Clem. 65:1), μετὰ καὶ ἑτέρων πολλῶν (Acts 15:35). This same idiom has been known to us from the papyri for half a century, as also from inscriptions.[9] Examples from the latter were pointed out in 1898 by W. H. P. Hatch.[10] (2) Hellenistic Greek shows evidence of using τε in the same superfluous way with particles or relative pronouns. This has been noted in Plutarch, not only as ὅς τε, etc., but as ἐπεί τε. Other writings agree in this usage and they also use τε with ἐάν, ἵνα, etc.[11] Though this phenomenon is doubtless an independent development, it suggests the same natural tendency that has led to the ὅς καί, ὡς καί, καθὼς καί, etc., of the New Testament and Hellenistic Greek.

[9] G. A. Deissmann, *Bible Studies*, pp. 265f. Wilhelm Schulze, *Zeitschrift für Vergleichende Sprachforschung* 33 (1895), 239–241.
[10] *Journal of Biblical Literature* 27, 142f.
[11] L. Radermacher, *Neutestamentliche Grammatik* (2d. ed., 1925) pp. 5f.

THE SOURCES OF PAULINE MYSTICISM

CHESTER CHARLTON McCOWN
Pacific School of Religion

I. NEED OF METHODOLOGY

History's chief attraction is "human interest." Its basic element is human experience. If the student of history is to proceed according to history's own version of scientific method, he must first collect data from experience; i.e., from concrete events, their relationships, and the human reactions to them. Only from such data can he proceed to generalizations and to the construction of hypotheses.

The historian, therefore, suffers a constant temptation to stress the particular as against the general, to emphasize discrete facts rather than co-ordinating principles. When he does generalize, the artist in him often displaces the scientist, and his conclusions tend to be naïve, casual, and emotional, rather than carefully considered and scientifically inductive. Consequently, before hypothesis hardens into theory and a "consensus of opinion" is established, it is imperative that a scientific methodology be developed and accepted. Certain basic principles must be adopted as to the techniques for gathering the various types of data and testing the resulting hypotheses upon which historical construction operates if any fairly permanent results are to be reached. Moreover, it must be recognized that no methodology can be regarded as final and perfect. Revision and improvement must always be sought, especially in a "science" so young and backward as historiography.

Many problems in the history of early Christianity suffer from a disconcerting lack of agreed solutions, primarily because of the failure to establish and revise methodological principles. One of these problems is the relation of Pauline mysticism to the mystery religions. From of old Paul's mysticism has usually been taken for granted as given directly from heaven and each school and sect has assumed that it has the correct interpretation of it. It need hardly be said, at this date, that any attempt to understand and interpret Paul is an historical undertaking. The sharp divergence of opinion that still prevails as to the nature of his mysticism [1] proves, however, that the type of historical method to be applied has not been carefully defined. Indeed, any semblance of method seems often to be wanting.

II. Purpose of Paper

This paper is an attempt to reach greater clarity in the matter. It is not so much an effort to solve the problem of the origins of Pauline mysticism, as rather an attempt to analyze it from a methodological point of view in order to discover the causes of the disagreements which separate the various schools of interpreters and then to suggest an evaluation of their arguments from the point of view of method.

The title, "Sources of Paul's Mysticism," it hardly need be said, does not refer to the causes of Paul's mystical experiences, but rather to the sources of his interpretations of his experiences, two very different matters, which, unhappily, are often confused. Paul's letters clearly demonstrate that he had certain emotional experiences which he understood to result from direct contact with God, or with the Spirit of God, or with the Spirit of Christ, to repeat some of his various expressions. However sadly men may

[1] Cf. Samuel Angus, *Religious Quests of the Graeco-Roman World* (New York, 1929), pp. 195 f.; J. Klausner, *From Jesus to Paul*, E.T. by W. F. Stinespring (New York, 1943), pp. 459–462; Ch. Guignebert, *Le Christ* (Paris, 1943), pp. 325–380; H. Weinel, *Biblische Theologie des neuen Testaments* (2d ed.; Tübingen, 1913), pp. 248–252; Cumont, *Les Religions orientales dans le paganisme romain* (4th ed.; Paris, 1929), pp. VIII–XIV, 206, note 2.

be deceived as to the causes of experiences such as he mentions — and Paul explicitly admits that one must try the spirits whether they be of God — the present paper is not concerned with psychological investigations or philosophical discussions of the origin and the veridical character of such experiences, but only with Paul's theories as to their meaning. The experiences, which are assumed to be of divine origin, are one thing; their meaning and value are quite another. Granted their reality, the interpretation of such experiences is theologically, socially, and ethically far more important than the experiences themselves. It is not the experience in itself but his interpretation of it which determines how the subject acts. It is not the voice heard, however soothing, or moving, or disturbing its sound may be, that directs the mob; it is what the mob understands the voice to say that counts. A command misunderstood may destroy a city.

Historically considered, Pauline mysticism has been extremely influential. Paul's mystical experiences were to him the very essence of his religion. Wherever so-called "Paulinism" prevails, and in the extent to which it prevails, experiences similar to Paul's are regarded as the only marks of a true Christian, and his interpretations of them are the basis of the only acceptable theology; all else is heterodoxy. Since Paul's experiences had a peculiarly vivid and unmistakable character, and his explanatory language was unusually colorful and suggestive, yet widely connotative rather than narrowly denotative, analogical rather than analytical, emotive rather than logical, he who pleaded hardest for Christian unity in the one body of Christ has been one of the chief sources of Christian disunity. The distinction, therefore, between his actual emotional experiences and the language in which he describes and interprets them is of prime importance, and a careful appraisal of his language is indispensable.

III. ROLE OF SOCIAL PATTERNS

Any interpretation of experience depends upon the thought categories or patterns which are used by the individual and which give form to his thought and to the language in which his emotions are expressed and described. Experiences of all kinds, as well as objects observed, receive meaning only when classified according to general notions, or patterns of thought. Patterns of thought, patterns of feeling, and patterns of action go together; the latter two are derived from the first. All are social products. Social patterns more than racial or physiological characteristics make the difference between the Englishman and the Italian. The "stoical Chinese," reared in the United States, may be as lively as an American. Not merely the expression of religious emotion, but the very emotion itself is deeply affected by current beliefs as to the effect of communion with God. The very experience of communion with God is made possible and colored and its character is determined by the individual's socially derived conceptions of God and of the nature of such an experience.

The origin of an idea or a pattern of ideas does not necessarily determine its values. The "fallacy of origins" must be avoided. Social patterns, like everything mundane, develop and deteriorate. An outstanding and original individual inevitably alters and adds to the current patterns of thought and action. Yet no effective individual rises far above his environment or differs radically from it. The general ideas and categories by which experience is classified are inevitably derived from the culture of the society to which a person belongs. He must speak approximately the language of his fellows if they are to understand him and accept his leadership. The meaning of the patterns of thought and of the words which any person uses is approximately that of the social groups in which he moves

THE SOURCES OF PAULINE MYSTICISM

and can be known by the discovery of their immediate sources. This paper is concerned with the discovery of the sources of the ideas which Paul expresses regarding his own mystical experiences and those of his fellow Christians.

This explicit statement of elementary principles seems necessary in view of the confusions which prevail in discussions of the subject. What has been said implies only that the meaning of Paul's language depends upon the culture to which he belongs. That is precisely the issue. Was he a Palestinian or a Diaspora Jew? Was ancient Hebrew culture as reinterpreted by rabbinism the chief ingredient in his thinking, or did he belong to the Hellenistic world? The essence of the problem, therefore, is a matter of cultural history. The special purpose of this essay is to analyze the problem in the light of cultural anthropology or cultural history, and, on this basis, to evaluate the various types of argument which have been put forward.

Anthropological, or, more precisely, ethnological method is invoked because recent studies in that field have dealt with problems of methodology in the area of cultural history with conspicuous clarity. Because of the attraction of "human interest," history long contented itself with actions of individuals. Because the individuals chiefly in the public eye and, therefore, of immediate "topical" interest were rulers and warriors, history was largely political and military. In religious history, particularly of New Testament times, the outstanding individuals, their activities, and their ideas, along with questions of organization and ritual, have too often monopolized attention. They have been studied *in vacuo*. The first step toward an accurate perspective, taken by Montesquieu and Voltaire, was the enlargement of history to include the culture of the society to which the individuals belonged.[2] The growth

[2] Cf. Robert Lowie, *The History of Ethnological Thought* (New York, 1937), pp. 10 f.

of attention to milieu marks the gradual development of a sociological point of view, which includes all classes of society and all features of human activity and thought, that is, the total stream of human experience, as the field of historical research.[3]

Unfortunately, cultural studies have too often been regarded merely as a backdrop for history. Actually, the only history that has scientific and normative value is cultural history. What the historian has called "continuity," and the ethnologist "functionalism," is an attempt to correct the individualist and episodical conception of history by discovering intercultural bonds and tracing cultural development.[4] Individuals, books, institutions, movements cannot be understood by themselves. Each is a function of the whole. History is a seamless garment. It represents both a time and a space continuum. Not only is history a process in time, evolutionary in its nature, but each event, in its measure, conditions every other contemporary as well as succeeding event, as the smallest asteroid affects the largest sun. The extent of gravitational effect is, in general, dependent on distance and mass. In cultural history much more subtle and complicated measurements are involved. The present task is to consider their nature and the necessary techniques in a particular case.

A study such as this has three main aspects: (1) the problem of method in intercultural studies as just outlined; (2) the question as to the nature of the New Testament documents and of the other sources, documentary and archaeological, available for the understanding of Paul's cultural situation, and (3) a comparison of the New Testament evidence regarding Paul with evidence regarding contemporary mysticism. Prejudice aside, the differences

---

[3] Cf. McCown, *The Search for the Real Jesus* (New York, 1940), pp. 112 ff., 124 f.

[4] *Op. cit.*, pp. 111–114; Lowie, *op. cit.*, 142 ff., 230–249, *et pas.*

THE SOURCES OF PAULINE MYSTICISM

of opinion which prevail are due chiefly to differences of procedure, or method, in all of these areas.

IV. Intercultural Relationships

No problem of intercultural relationships can be stated without at once raising the question of "borrowing," a word which has a pejorative connotation. More precisely expressed, it is a question of "diffusion *vs.* parallelism," a subject which recalls a long and unedifying quarrel among anthropologists and students of religions. One theory is that mankind was, and is, naturally inventive, and that, under fairly similar circumstances, the psychic unity of the race produces the discovery of similar ideas and techniques in widely separated regions of the world. The contrary theory is that man is uninventive and that the basic ideas and techniques which make culture have been discovered once for all by specially gifted individuals under favorable circumstances (or have been divinely revealed), and have then spread over all the world.

Both theories have been so exaggerated by their proponents as to prejudice opinion against them, and reaction has swung violently first to one and then to the other extreme. The English diffusionists, led by Elliot Smith and W. J. Perry, cast discredit upon their theory by "unfathomable ignorance of elementary ethnography" and conspicuous inability to treat their evidence objectively.[5] Consequently, there was a strong reaction toward reliance upon independent, parallel discovery and development. However, the present tendency is to strike a balance between extremes. Pan-Babylonianism and Pan-Egyptianism are equally mistaken. Ideas and customs may arise independently, sometimes from similar, sometimes from diverse, antecedents. It is impossible to "deny all significant origi-

[5] Lowie, *op. cit.*, pp. 167, 169.

nality to mankind at large" and "limit it to the ancient Egyptians" or the ancient Sumerians. Yet innumerable striking examples of the spread of ideas, myths, customs, and inventions prove that within the Americas and within the Eurasian-African land mass alike, diffusion has been the rule.

Parallel development may be considered when cultures are oceans apart, but not when they are in intimate contact. As innumerable examples, ancient and modern, conclusively prove, intercultural contacts inevitably lead to mutual borrowings, adaptations, and imitations, and eventually to cultural syntheses. Even the culture which regards itself, and indeed is, superior in richness and complexity is eventually affected. Diffusion, or intercultural exchange, has been the rule, rather than the exception.[6]

Moreover, one conclusion from the study of cultural relations is especially in point in the present connection. While an old and rich culture may sometimes be swallowed up or destroyed by an invasion of a more primitive and physically more vigorous people, intercultural cross-fertilization is one of the chief causes of cultural progress. The idea of the superiority of pure races and pure cultures is pure nonsense. Borrowing is as valuable in the growth of cultures as in the development of business enterprises. The primitive people which appeared to overwhelm and blot out its older preceding culture often appropriated that which it appeared to destroy and produced a better civilization. No culture lives long unto itself. Any which does so dies by itself. Isolation, whether geographical or political or ideological, whether self-imposed or forced from without, inevitably results in deterioration. No better example could be found than the medieval, and modern, Ghetto. The most highly developed cultures have, in general, been those which had the greatest number of intercultural contacts and

[6] A. L. Kroeber, *Anthropology* (New York, 1923), pp. 194–292; Lowie, *op. cit.*, pp. 251 f.

which succeeded best in adapting and assimilating cultural values from others.

In such interchanges everything depends upon the manner in which the borrowed trait is used. No stigma should attach to borrowing; it is the use of the borrowed materials that counts. The assimilation of a foreign culture trait is, essentially, not the act of an individual, but a social process. Many factors condition the attractiveness and use of a trait: its utility, its adaptability, and also its intellectual or aesthetic or dramatic appeal.[7] The borrowed object or pattern is almost never taken over whole, at least not by a vigorous and developing civilization. Depending upon the similarity of the two cultures concerned, and the vitality of the borrower, it will be reshaped and improved by the borrower.

A. L. Kroeber has recently given to a peculiarly original type of adaptation the name of "stimulus diffusion," or "idea diffusion." A system, or pattern, is usually taken over with certain items of its content. In "stimulus diffusion" the content is entirely rejected; only the system, or idea, is adopted. One of the best and most familiar examples is the adaptation of Egyptian hieroglyphics to the Hebrew-Phoenician alphabet. The scheme of reducing spoken speech to signs was given an entirely new and epoch-making usefulness when it was applied, not to the representation of ideas or syllables, but, by a new and abstract analysis, to the component parts of syllables.[8] The concept of stimulus diffusion seems particularly applicable to the early Christian and Pauline use of Hellenistic religions.

The pertinence of these conclusions to the problem of Pauline mysticism is evident. It is a matter of intercultural

[7] Cf. Wilson D. Wallis, *An Introduction to Sociology* (New York, 1927), pp. 373–379; *Culture and Progress* (New York, 1930), pp. 77–106.
[8] Cf. Kroeber, "Stimulus Diffusion," *American Anthropologist*, N.S., 42 (1940), 1–20; and numerous illustrations in his *Configurations of Culture Growth* (Berkeley, 1944), p. 201 et pas.; McCown, *The Ladder of Progress in Palestine* (New York, 1943), p. 114.

relations. More fully stated the question at issue is how the clash of Jewish and Hellenistic cultures affected the development of Christianity. It began as a thoroughly Jewish messianic movement based upon Old Testament prophecy and Jewish apocalyptic eschatology. Its central feature was the hope of a social transformation which was to be wrought by the miraculous intervention of God and which should establish on earth economic justice, class equality, and individual righteousness, with resulting universal well being and happiness. Oppressors were to be overthrown, the oppressed set free, and social derelicts saved. All evil was to come to an end. Within two or three generations this Jewish movement concerned with righteousness and justice in the present world had been transformed into a universalistic, mystical, semimagical, otherworldly cult of a heavenly Kyrios. Chiefly by means of its cultic rites according to popular belief, the new religion sought individual salvation from sin and eventual immortality and was largely alien to its original social intention and interest. Whether "the powers that be" were hostile to God or ordained by Him, social righteousness in this world was not important. Salvation lay finally only in another world. The immediate question as to the part Paul played in this transformation can be answered only by discovering the meaning of his language, and that is to be found by determining the sources of the terms he used to describe his experience and his application of them. Was he using the language and ideas of a Palestinian rabbi or of a Jew of the Hellenistic Dispersion?

V. Contemporary Evidence

The answers to these questions are to be found in contemporary documents, the New Testament and the literary and nonliterary remains as well as the archaeological materials regarding popular religious beliefs, Jewish and Hellenistic, and especially regarding the mystery cults of the first

THE SOURCES OF PAULINE MYSTICISM 59

century. As to the New Testament, it should hardly be necessary to state that the only trustworthy source of information regarding Paul is to be found in Paul's own letters. This is not the place in which to discuss the historical value of the Book of Acts.[9] Great as that value is, it must be remembered that Paul's letters are primary sources, the Book of Acts definitely secondary as regards the first generation of Christians, including Paul himself. Moreover, practically every statement in Acts emphasizing Paul's Jewishness is in the fictional "Thucydidean" speeches of Acts and, therefore, is doubly under suspicion.[10] The irenic and apologetic motifs in Acts easily account for the author's assumptions that there was little difference between Jewish and Gentile Christianity. Paul's own letters, on the contrary, even in the passages which emphasize his Jewishness, where references to Gamaliel and an education at Jerusalem might be expected, make no such claims. Actually they are quite ambiguous, except as to his ancestry.

Paul did, indeed, claim to have been a strict Pharisee. What his standards of observance were we cannot know. His claims are general, without definite content. Even so, it is perfectly clear that it was against the Pharisaic conception of salvation by observing the Law that he bitterly rebelled. For Paul salvation from the Law, that is from Judaism, was as important as salvation from sin. He insisted, moreover, that his new faith was the true Judaism. With a shout of relief he exclaims that he had abandoned all his Jewishness and thrown it away as offal in order that he might be a true Christian.[11] The question as to what he

---

[9] Cf. recent "introductions"; also D. W. Riddle, *Paul, Man of Conflict* (Nashville, 1940), pp. 187–200.

[10] Acts 22:3 ff.; 23:3–10; 24:10–18; 25:8; 26:2–5. Acts 9:26–30; 11:27–30; 15:1–29 are in part contradicted by Paul's own statements (Gal. 1:18–2:2). Acts 9:3–7; 22:6–11; 26:12–19, the accounts of Paul's conversion, show the author's freedom in transmitting the traditions, probably oral, of the early period.   [11] 2 Cor. 11:22; Phil. 3:5–9; cf. Gal. 1:3 f.; Rom. 7:7–8:1.

threw away and what he retained can be answered only from what Paul reveals as to his Christian beliefs.

The authentic Jewish element in Paul must neither be minimized nor magnified. It is comparatively easy for the Christian scholar to discover it, perhaps too easy, for appearances in this matter are frequently deceptive. Paul often argues like a rabbi. But allegory and strained interpretations had been applied to Homer, Hesiod, and Greek mythology in general long before Hellenistic times. Such methods of evasion were especially prized by the Stoics. They were widely used by Jews of the Diaspora, notoriously by Philo.[12] Paul's most distinctive Jewish trait was his eschatology, which, before him, had been adapted from Magianism and which he in part assimilated to Hellenistic ideas of immortality. His ethics and his theology are not un-Jewish, but, in many points, they have marked affinities with Stoicism, as have his methods of exegesis. Stoicism and Judaism often agreed.

The decisive evidence as to Paul's cultural atmosphere is to be found, not in what he thought he was and claimed to be, but in what his own words unconsciously reveal him to have been. The year 1943 saw the publication of two works by competent scholars who emphatically claim Paul to have been, not the true Pharisaic Hebrew he evidently thought himself to be (2 Cor. 11:22; Phil. 3:4ff.), but a thoroughly Hellenized Diaspora Jew. When two scholars so radically different in their critical and religious presuppositions as Charles Guignebert and Joseph Klausner agree that Paul's Christianity was thoroughly un-Jewish and diverged sharply from the religion of Jesus, the significance of their thesis cannot be lightly overlooked.[13] The opinion

[12] See, for example, W. Schmidt in W. von Christ's *Geschichte der griechischen Litteratur* (6th ed.; Munich, 1912, 1920), I, 82, 85, and notes 9 f., 129; II, 631 f., 652–656; W. Bousset, *Religion des Judentums im späthellen. Zeitalter* (3d ed.; Tübingen, 1926), p. 161.

[13] Guignebert, *Le Christ*, pp. 1–12, 356 f.; Klausner, *From Jesus to Paul*,

THE SOURCES OF PAULINE MYSTICISM

of a highly competent Jewish scholar, like Rabbi Klausner, as to the Jewishness of Paul, carries especial weight.

It is Paul's faith-mysticism, his conception, not of God's character, but of the Christian's relation to God, in which he departs most radically from Palestinian Judaism and approaches views found in Philo, approaches only to pass far beyond in the direction of Hermetism and the later pagan mysticism of Plotinus and Porphyry. Could this element be derived from the Old Testament, the later apocalyptic and apocryphal Jewish literature, or rabbinic teaching as illustrated in the Talmud, or is it to be explained as due to Hellenistic influence?

VI. THE HELLENISTIC MYSTERY RELIGIONS

To determine the extent and meaning of the non-Jewish element in Paul's thought, his language must be compared with that of the mystery religions. The possibility that he was thoroughly familiar with the chief ideas of the Hellenistic religions cannot be questioned. It may be admitted that the most important documents which treat them with some fullness come from the second century or later. Apuleius' *Golden Ass*, with its instructive accounts of Isiac initiations, Plutarch's *Isis and Osiris*, the majority of the Mithraic monuments, the Poimandres and Hermetic literature, all belong after Paul's time. It may be granted that before the Christian era detailed information regarding the mystery religions, especially those of oriental origin, is wanting. Indeed, we know too little from any period. But the ancient and widespread cult of Dionysus, the mysteries of Samothrace and Eleusis, with the Orphic interpretations of their rites, antedate Christianity by many centuries. Adonis, Attis and Magna Mater, Osiris and Isis, and

---

pp. 450–466, who uses Acts uncritically and, therefore, reaches the conclusion (p. 466) that Paul's basic ideas were Jewish, but colored by Hellenism.

Mithra himself are attested as deities worshiped with mystery rites long before Paul was born.[14] The absence of fuller literary evidence proves nothing. Allusions are enough. The modern student, accustomed to learning solely from books, is prone to assume that, in ancient times as in modern, new ideas were propagated in writing. When a few copies of any document were laboriously made by hand and read only by a minute minority of the population, a new faith was necessarily propagated by word of mouth. Preaching came first with other missionaries besides Paul and his co-laborers. The gospel was before the Gospels. Later written documents appeared in order that converts might know the certainty of the things in which they had been instructed (Lk. 1:1). First the spoken, then the written, word was the natural order. The mystery cults, since they were secret, would have been all the more chary of written documents.[15] As they were eventually defeated and destroyed by victorious Christianity, they suffered the fate of the vanquished, oblivion. Their few records were neglected when not intentionally destroyed. Absence of numerous contemporary documents is immaterial. If it were decisive, the existence of Christianity in the first century would be in doubt.

Asia Minor, where Paul was born, and where Christianity enjoyed its first large successes, was especially notable as the home of synthetic cults as well as mystery religions. They could not have been unknown at Tarsus, a seaport lying at the opening of the Cilician Gates, the great pathway from Orient to Occident. Long before Paul was born the Cilician pirates worshiped Mithra, who may already have been a mystery deity. Sandan, the chief god of Tarsus,

---

[14] See the discussion of dates in H. R. Willoughby, *Pagan Regeneration* (Chicago, 1929), pp. 39 f., 109, 149, 184, 198–202.

[15] Well illustrated by the fragmentary character of the Orphic "tablets" found in Italy and Crete.

THE SOURCES OF PAULINE MYSTICISM 63

was a vegetation deity who, apparently, died, went to heaven and was restored to life each year, and who, therefore, was at least an apt candidate for a mystery cult.[16]

Not all Jews were deeply impregnated with pagan elements, but Hellenistic Jewish literature gives significant evidence as to the effects of constant contacts with foreign culture upon men who believed themselves true Jews. The Wisdom of Solomon and Philo's works are only the best known of a large number, many preserved only by title. Paul certainly knew the former. He may have heard the name of Philo; hardly more. Yet Philo and similar Jewish apologists for their faith go far to make clear the kind of influences which were constantly at work upon Jews of the Hellenistic Dispersion. In all probability the influence of such works, many now long ago lost, as well as direct contact with Hellenistic ideas that were current in the workshop and the market place, were responsible for a conditioning of Paul's mind and spirit of which he was quite unconscious. If he persecuted Hellenistic Jewish Christians in Damascus and elsewhere, their defenses of their faith would have worked upon him the more effectively because of his resistance to their arguments. Paul was not the only or the first converted Diaspora Jew.[17] Quite the contrary. In many ways he reaped where he had not sowed. In spite of himself he built on others' foundations.

Wherever Paul's restless urge to evangelize the heathen took him he would have come upon votaries of the mystery cults, either Greek or Oriental. Adonis was famous in Syria. Anatolia, where Paul traveled more widely, spent more time, and wrote more letters than anywhere else, so

[16] Hans Böhlig, *Die Geisteskultur von Tarsus im augusteischen Zeitalter* (Göttingen, 1913), pp. 44–57, 92–107.
[17] Cf. Guignebert, *Le Christ*, pp. 189–200, 259–266; E. R. Goodenough, *By Light, Light* (New Haven, 1935).

far as the records of Acts go, was especially the home of syncretistic Jewish cults, such as that of Sabazios.[18] Phrygia was noted for its cults (and became the first great stronghold of Christianity). At Ephesus Paul must have observed the numerous Magna Mater shrines that still may be seen, as well as the famous Artemision. He is said to have passed through Samothrace (Acts 16:11). In Philippi and Thessalonika could he have failed to hear of the Dionysiac orgies of the women of Macedonia? At Athens and Corinth he could hardly have argued regarding the resurrection without hearing of Eleusis and Persephone. Everywhere he would learn of mysteries taught only the "perfect," or "mature," that is to "initiates" (*teleioi*).[19] In the middle of the first centuries, in any of the cities which Paul visited, it is impossible that the mass of the inhabitants, whether themselves initiates or not, should have been ignorant of what the mystery religions promised. It is equally impossible that a person so keen of perception and appreciative of current thinking as Paul's letters show him to have been, a man who prided himself on being all things to all men, should have ignored this competition and the positive religious values of the competing religions. Men everywhere were seeking and being promised salvation from evil and escape from an evil world into a happy immortality through fellowship with deities who had overcome evil and death by themselves dying and rising again. He could not fail to respond to such needs.

VII. Paul's Use of Mystery Language

When Paul's cultural relations are considered, it is not at all strange that his letter to the Colossians (1:26f., 2:2)

---

[18] Cumont, *op. cit.* (above, note 1), pp. 59–71.
[19] 1 Cor. 2:6, 13:10, 14:20; Phil. 3:15; not always with a mystery connotation.

THE SOURCES OF PAULINE MYSTICISM 65

should speak of the long-hidden "mystery which is Christ in you, the hope of glory," of the "recognition of the mystery of God, Christ, in whom are hidden all the treasures of wisdom and knowledge" (*sophia* and *gnosis*), and should warn most vehemently against what are apparently theosophic, gnostic, and ascetic cults of elemental spirits and angels. The word "mystery" appears again and again in Paul's letters, usually in connection with the idea of the revelation of divine wisdom and with that of the indwelling Christ, or the Spirit.[20] Paul's hearers and readers could hardly have missed, what must also have been in his own mind, the overtones of reference to the revelations in initiations into the mystery religions, or perchance to the ideas of Hermetism.

In Paul's scattered and unsystematized interpretations and expositions of his faith in Christ, what he offers is a series of attempts to make Christianity intelligible and attractive to people who were fully acquainted with the promises of salvation through union with a deity in a mystery cult. He uses illustration after illustration, drawn sometimes from life, but more often from the language of the cults,[21] to prove that faith in Christ guaranteed all that any mystery cult could promise, and very much more. Jesus Christ had died and risen again; he was a heavenly *Kyrios*, like the "lords" of the mystery cults, and like them a *Soter*, a "Savior." The Christian was "baptized into his death, . . . grown together (*symphytos*) with him in the likeness of his death, but also of his resurrection" (Rom. 6:3 ff.). Even more significant is the famous saying, "I am crucified with Christ, and I no longer live, but Christ lives in me" (Gal. 2:19 f.).

This is neither Judaism nor the religion of the synoptic

[20] 1 Cor. 2:7, 4:1, 13:2, 14:2, 15:51; Rom. 11:25, 16:25.
[21] Examples in Adolf Deissmann, *Licht vom Osten* (4th ed.; Tübingen, 1923), pp. 214–334 (chap. IV).

Gospels nor that of Jesus.[22] On the other hand, it is anything but pure mystery-cult doctrine. Paul is confident that his mystical relationship with Christ guarantees his future resurrection (Rom. 8:11); the gift of the Spirit is an *arrabon*, a "pledge," of eternal life (2 Cor. 1:22; 5:5). But, quite in contrast to anything that we know of the mystery religions, the divine life imparted to the soul meant a new moral life (Rom. 6:4–15, 8:12 f.). The passage often quoted to prove Paul a sacramentarian (1 Cor. 11:27–30) demonstrates just the opposite. The eucharist is a sacred thing. But it does not save *ex opere operato*; just the contrary. God will punish him who partakes unworthily.[23] Both faith-mysticism and morality enter into the operation.

This is perhaps sufficient to illustrate the attitudes and methods which promise most for an understanding of Paul's part in the development of Christian thought. He is to be seen as the child of two conflicting heritages: the practical, activist, this-worldly, ethical, legalistic, nonspeculative attitudes of Judaism, on the one hand, and, on the other, the imaginative, speculative, ascetic, at times amoral, mystical tendencies of Hellenism. He combined the two in an unstable compound which was very different from the religion of Jesus and equally different from any of the mystery religions or ethical philosophies of Hellenism. As Guignebert has forcibly expressed it, the Diaspora Jew, Paul, torn between the warring Jewish and Hellenistic elements which his mixed social origin had implanted in him, found in Christianity regarded as a doctrine of salvation "the harmonization of his unconscious aspirations as an Asiatic and his hopes as a Jew." [24]

Paul's descriptions of his Christian faith are the attempts

---

[22] Cf. Klausner's reaction to "this strange faith based on such unnatural beliefs," *From Jesus to Paul*, p. 495.
[23] Cf. Guignebert, *Le Christ*, pp. 374 f.
[24] *Le Christ*, p. 266.

THE SOURCES OF PAULINE MYSTICISM 67

of a peculiarly gifted and receptive spirit to put, into understandable language and familiar, contemporary thought forms, ideas which would satisfy the religious needs of his fellow seekers after salvation as he felt them in himself and observed them in others. The result is a social product, the product of the impact of Hellenistic culture upon Jewish-Persian culture and upon generations of Diaspora Jews before Jesus and Paul were born. Paul's religious faith is not an autonomous, independent development. His mysticism is neither a "parallel development" to Hellenistic mysticism, nor a borrowed idea, taken over unchanged, but the result of "stimulus diffusion": i.e., it is Jewish trust in Yahweh and Jewish belief in divine inspiration as illustrated in the prophets expressed in the framework, the thought categories and the language, of the mystery religions. Prophetic ethical monotheism is presented with the social pattern of pagan mysticism.[25]

Paul was clearly "borrowing" from the religions of his environment. But what was borrowed was immediately put out at high interest, or, to use another figure, the seed fell into fertile soil and bore fruit an hundredfold. It is a clear case of "stimulus diffusion," in which a new content, related but different, was put into another system. It was a departure on a long journey, from the social "good tidings of God's reign" to the individualistic hope of salvation from sin and an evil world to eternal life in heaven. But it met the needs of a great population which lived under very different cultural conditions and had very different religious desires from those of Jesus' hearers. Without the transformation which Christianity suffered at the hands of Paul Christianity could hardly have survived in the Roman Empire.

[25] As Professor Hatch has put it, Paul's mysticism was absorbed from his environment; *The Pauline Idea of Faith* (Cambridge, 1917), p. 66.

POST-PAULINE PAULINISM

BURTON SCOTT EASTON
General Theological Seminary

In terms of the "classical" New Testament Theology the characteristics of Paulinism may be summarized as follows: —

(a) Justification by faith only. At the moment a man surrenders his heart to Christ he receives from God complete pardon for all his sins; and as long as he continues in that faith his further sins are not reckoned against him. And this justification is solely by faith; works play no part in it.

(b) Sanctification by the Spirit. Positive growth in what we call "holiness" (Paul uses the word rather differently to describe a technical religious status) is produced by God's gift of the Spirit to the believing soul. But, since the Spirit is given through Christ, there is a union of Christ with the soul, so that sanctification may likewise be said to come from this union.

(c) Baptism. According to Romans 6:3–6, Colossians 2:11–12, this union with Christ is accomplished at baptism. It is then that "the body of sin is done away," "the body of flesh is put off," in order that "walking in newness of life" may be possible. Logically therefore complete Christian salvation is accomplished in two steps separated in time: the first confession of faith, which brings pardon, and baptism, which confers the Spirit and the union with Christ. But since in the apostolic age baptism was administered immediately on profession of faith, the state of the soul in the interim raised no problem worthy of consideration.

(d) The death of Christ. In Pauline thought this is utilized in many different connections; usually however by allusion rather than in concrete doctrinal terms. As an "Atonement," in the ordinary sense of the word, Paul formulates no precise definition; but of the theories developed in later theology perhaps the Abelardian comes closest; "we were reconciled to God through the death of his son" (Rom. 5:10). But in Galatians and Colossians Paul sets forth explicitly the teaching that the Cross was Christ's victory over the aeons (*stoicheia*) hostile to men.

(e) The destruction of the Law. This is basic in Paul's thinking and is supported by several arguments. The victory over the aeons was a victory over the Law, for the aeons gave the Law (Gal. 4:5, Col. 2:15, etc.). Christ by defying the curse of the Law showed it to be futile and swept it aside (Gal. 3:13, etc.). Most familiar, however, is the contention that the Law was unable to accomplish God's plan of salvation (Rom. 3:20, etc.); a different method accordingly had to be provided. As the Law is one and indivisible its repeal is total, with no distinction between "moral" and "ceremonial" precepts. So to the Christian the Old Testament has value only because of its prophecies.

(f) The equality of all believers. As the Law is abolished all legal Jewish privileges have gone with it, so there is in Christ neither Jew nor Greek; no barbarian, Scythian, bond or free; not even male or female; all are one in Christ. None the less, Paul cannot help feeling that Jews have at least a certain start in the race; when asked "what advantage has the Jew?" he replies "much in every way." And yet in his further discussion he is unable to give this "much" appreciable content; it really reduces to his prediction that the Jews will eventually be restored.

(g) A simplified basis for conduct. The Christians' sole law is the law of love. The resulting ethic, Paul claims, is vastly superior to the old legalism; in addition to being incomparably more adaptable to new problems, it permits a far fuller and more joyous activity.

There are, of course, many more aspects to Paul's thought, particularly as regards his Christology, but the seven themes recapitulated form "Paulinism" in the technical and controversial sense. And it is to their complex that he gives the title "Gospel." So familiar is this word to the later Christian mind that we often forget that it does not belong to the primitive Christian vocabulary; it was introduced as a technical — or even polemical — term by Paul. This Gospel is the true "good news," which the Apostle did not receive from men but which came to him by revelation from Jesus Christ. And this "news" is "good" because it teaches men that they now can have peace with God and can rejoice in the hope of the glory of God, rejoice with a hope that putteth not to shame.

Paul does not of course mean that full acceptance of his teaching is necessary for salvation. When he writes to the Romans he writes as to fellow-heirs of the Kingdom, who have as fully put on Christ as has he himself. But he wishes his readers to realize, as fully as does he himself, the immensity of the riches of their inheritance; he writes to rid their consciences of timid scrupulosity, that in going on to the high goal to which they have been called they may go on joyously and triumphantly.

Contemporary students of Paulinism are past doubt right in maintaining that the above "classical" reconstruction of the Apostle's theology is too logical and systematic; the Jewish mind — which Paul possessed without qualification — did not think in such closed categories. The letters, moreover, are "occasional" writings in the strictest sense; not only the problems presented but Paul's attitude toward those problems are created by the occasion, with the result that self-contradictions are by no means rare. In Galatians and Colossians, for instance, the inadequacy of the Law is explained by arguing that its givers were the angelic aeons, while in Romans — although not only in Romans — it is roundly called "the Law of God" (7:22, 25; 8:7). In 1 Thessalonians 2:15–16 there is an outburst of passionate anti-Semitism, proclaiming that the wrath has come on the

Jews to the uttermost, while in Romans 11 we read that in God's appointed time all Israel shall be saved. And even in the course of a single Epistle there are conflicts; as in Galatians, where in 3:2 we read of receiving the Spirit by "the hearing of faith," although a little later in the same chapter (*v.* 27) Christ is said to be "put on" at baptism. Such inconsistencies are by no means few and they doubtless could be multiplied if other letters of Paul had been preserved; perhaps vastly multiplied if we had records of all he taught orally throughout his long career. None the less, the "classical" analysis adequately presents Paul as he was best known to his contemporaries and summarizes the teachings for which he was praised or blamed.

Not all the elements of his doctrine were controversial; not even when they were novel or when they gave a new significance to accepted beliefs. According to the evidence of Acts — which in this instance may be wholly trusted — in the first days of Christianity little or no soteriological significance was attached to the death of Christ; this was preached simply as an atrocious crime of the Jews, which God had overruled. Just so Paul, in his own "minimal" summary of Christian belief in Romans 10:9, gives only confession of Christ's Lordship and faith in his resurrection as fully sufficient to win salvation. Yet even without Paul's influence some type of Atonement teaching was bound to emerge; the figure of Isaiah's Suffering Servant, for instance, was inescapable in even the most Jewish type of Christian thinking. So Paul's emphasis on the Cross would in itself have been most welcome, even though perhaps not in all its aspects; all the more because his very lack of dogmatic precision permitted other thinkers, such as the writer of Hebrews, to develop their own systems as they pleased.

Wholly welcome also was his teaching about the Spirit, which simply carried on and expanded what was already held universally. To be sure, his conception of the Spirit establishing the mystical union with Christ doubtless fell on many deaf ears; the mystic is never comprehensible to the non-mystic. But no one would quarrel with Paul because of his mysticism.

As regards baptism Paul won a signal triumph; a triumph all the greater because his teaching seems to have prevailed without trace of opposition. In the first Palestinian Christianity as recorded in Acts — whose evidence here again may be wholly trusted — baptism was regarded precisely as in non-Christian Judaism as a washing away of past sins (Acts 22:16) with no accompanying gift of the Spirit (8:16). This gift was wholly independent of baptism; it might be bestowed without human mediation (10:44; 18:25 — noting here that the correct translation is "fervent in the Spirit"), but normally was conveyed by the Old Testament rite (Deuteronomy 34:9) of imposing hands, either before (Acts 9:17) or after (8:17; 19:6) baptism. But in the post-Pauline references to baptism except perhaps 1 Peter 3:21 it is invariably assumed that the gift of the Spirit is bestowed in the rite itself (Titus 3:5; John 3:5); a belief definitely confirmed when the older form of baptism in the name of Christ was displaced by the trine formula including the name of the Spirit. And when the later baptismal liturgies developed, they one and all contained prayers or ceremonies for the gift of the Spirit on the person baptized. In fact the triumph of Paul's doctrine of baptism was so complete as to suggest that the triumph was rather one of Hellenistic than of specifically Pauline concepts; there is much in the early Christian history of baptism that is still obscure.

It was around the other elements of Paulinism that controversies developed. In the forefront of course was his teaching about justification. Paul, to be sure, insisted that this teaching was not innovation; in Galatians 2:16 he tells us that he used "faith in Christ, not works of the Law" as common ground in his dispute with Peter, as a Christian axiom which they both accepted. And there was much reason in his contention. From the very beginning faith in Christ was regarded as the all-essential quality; a sinful woman who had this faith could be assured of salvation while the most virtuous Jew who rejected Christ could not. And yet the sharp Pauline antithesis of "faith not works" was disturbing; it was so patently capable of distortion if held as an isolated dogma.

Just so Paul's doctrine of the destruction of the Law was patently capable of distortion if held as an isolated dogma and capable of even greater distortion if combined with the "faith not works" antithesis. But in any form the doctrine of the destruction of the Law must have appalled devout Jewish Christians; when they first heard it it would have impressed them as nothing short of blasphemy. There had been no preparation for so revolutionary an innovation; Jesus had quarrelled with scribal perversions of the Law but never with the Law as such. To the Jewish mind the Law and righteousness were inseparable; they were one and the same thing; obedience to the Law was not the way to righteousness but was righteousness itself. If virtues could be attributed to a Gentile, they were due to the fact that in those virtues the Gentile was unconsciously practicing what the Law commanded. And now to be told that this was all wrong; that the Law, even though good, was a source of evil — Paul's teaching in Romans; or, worse, that the Law had not been given by God at all — Paul's teaching in Galatians and Colossians; such teaching could not be condemned too hotly or too completely.

Amid this resentment Paul's argument that a higher Christian ethic could be developed from the law of love would not have received a fair hearing. It was perfectly true, of course, that Paul here was wholly faithful to the teaching of Jesus, who had summed up the whole Law in love of God and love of neighbor. This could not be denied nor did the Jewish Christians wish to deny it, for they too proclaimed their Master's summary with pride. But they proclaimed it as a summary, to be amplified with the laws that make up the Law; not as the foundation of a fresh start, in which all the past should be swept aside.

Did it follow, however, that the entire Law was of obligation on all Christians? From the standpoint of rigorous Jewish logic this would appear axiomatic and Acts tells us that certain extremists actually so maintained (15:1, 5). But even in non-Christian Judaism there were many who held a more tolerant point of view toward at least certain Gentiles; the numerous "God-fearers" or "God-worshippers" who were attached to synagogues all over the empire and who worshipped the God of Israel and — perhaps not an anti-climax — gave much alms to the people. If no hope at all had been held out to these persons, their continuance is hardly explicable. There was no doubt no formulated theology regarding their status, for closely formulated theology of any kind was foreign to Judaism, but their eventual fate must have been held to be far better than that of Gentiles who continued in idolatry; far, far better than that of Gentiles who persecuted the Jews.

The Jewish Christian attitude to similar Gentiles who not only worshipped the God of Israel but who accepted Christ necessarily must have been not only more tolerant still but must have included definite assurance of salvation. And this quite independently of any teaching by Paul, who was by no means the only missionary to the Gentiles. The elaborate account of Peter's work with Cornelius and his friends in Acts cannot be taken at its full face value, for it is quite impossible to reconcile Acts 11:3 with Galatians 2:12; still some beginning of Gentile work in Palestine by Peter may very well lie behind the story. More reliable is the account of the beginnings of Gentile work in Antioch by certain men of Cyprus and Cyrene in 11:20-21. But the fullest proof is offered by Romans; here was a Gentile community which had come into existence through no efforts of Paul or his disciples; which in fact was ignorant and even suspicious of his theology. And the number of similar non-Pauline Gentile communities was obviously greater than the positive New Testament evidence indicates.

Such progress must have received the full endorsement of Palestinian Christianity. So we may doubt the significance, if not the very existence, of an intransigent group of Jewish Christians insisting on circumcision for all believers. There is no trace of them in Paul's letters. In Galatians the theme is not the possibility of Gentile salvation but of Gentile equality; what Paul assails is the folly of seeking "perfection" in the flesh after beginning in the Spirit. And we may ask if in Acts 15 Luke has not smoothed over the controversy by making it turn on a point on which there was no real disagreement, so as to display perfect harmony between Paul and the Jerusalemites. What actually underlies the story of the "Apostolic Council" is probably beyond complete recovery but the decree perhaps states Jerusalem's minimum terms on which Jews and Gentiles could eat together; a vital problem in a religion in which the central act of worship was a common meal.

This acceptance by the Palestinian church of the brotherhood of Gentile Christians without binding them to full observance of the Law had, however, a significant reaction on the Jewish Christian estimate of the Law. While all Jews accepted the fully divine origin of every individual precept in the Pentateuch, they never regarded them all of equal weight; all teachers held that certain precepts were "light" and others "heavy." In Judaism proper this distinction had never been made along the lines of "ceremonial" and "moral" but the effect of the Gentile mission was to bring Christian Judaism to just about this conclusion. In so doing they had the additional stimulus from the teaching of Jesus, who had taught consistently that in any conflict between a ceremonial and a moral law the former must give way (Mk. 2:25–26; 7:9–13; Mt. 5:23–24; 12:7; Lk. 13:15–16, etc.). It could therefore be logically argued that the principle "mercy, not sacrifice" could very well be applied to Gentiles who believed in Christ. To be sure, the problem had complications, for the distinction between "ceremonial" and "moral" raises further problems of its own when applied to the multitudinous precepts of the Law; in various cases a wide margin of dispute was possible. It seems to have been agreed on all hands, for instance, that Sabbath observance was ceremonial, but while Paul rated eating things sacrificed to idols among the *adiaphora* the Palestinians contended passionately that the prohibition was moral to the last degree. Yet such differences in details did not affect the general principle; as long as the Gentile believers accepted the righteousness taught by the Law, Jewish Christians were content.

Still, of course, from the Jewish standpoint such observers of this minimum requirement occupied in the church a position inferior to those who observed the Law in its entirety; all the more because to the Jewish mind the superiority of the Israelite over the non-Israelite was an axiom which even Paul himself accepted. The Jerusalemites would look on the Gentile converts much as missionaries look on converts in central Africa; fellow Christians no doubt but for whom a guiding hand must never be relaxed. The rapid spread of the church throughout the Empire and beyond was a cause for Palestinian rejoicing — but the central authority must always remain in Palestine and more specifically in Jerusalem. So thought the Jewish Christians and so perhaps at first thought certain of the Gentile Christians. But it could not be long before the latter thought differently; the teaching of Paul on Gentile equality attracted them as definitely as it repelled the Palestinians.

The elements of Paulinism then that were to become controversial were these: (a) His justification doctrine, especially in its sharp "faith, not works" antithesis. This was difficult to understand as he stated it and was capable of grotesque distortion. (b) The total repeal of the Law. Jewish Christians rejected this altogether; the attitude of Gentile Christians will be studied below. (c) The equality of Jew and Gentile in Christ. This Jewish Christians likewise rejected, while it was to become a Gentile Christian dogma. Involved in the whole dispute was the question of Paul's authority; was he, as he claimed, a full apostle in his own right, independent of the Twelve and coordinate with them — or even in virtue of his special revelations their superior? Was what he called the "Gospel" the truest expression of Christian belief?

That his authority and teaching met with immediate and bitter opposition is amply evidenced by his letters in a long list of familiar passages (Gal. 1:8-10; 1 Cor. 15:8; 2 Cor. 12:16, Phil. 1:15-17, etc.). Nor can we dismiss this opposition merely by calling his enemies "Judaizers" and forgetting them. When 2 Timothy 1:15 tells that "all that are in Asia have turned away from me," the writer of the Pastorals is certainly not drawing on his own invention; this writer certainly knew Acts (2 Tim. 3:11) and could not have been unconscious of the poignant contrast between his statement about the Asians and that in Acts 20:36-38. Yet of the details of the opposition we have no specific information; no explicitly anti-Pauline writing has survived — or could, probably, be expected to survive.

The Jewish Christian standpoint is preserved in Matthew's Gospel, where the Christian ideal is not merely observance of the Law but actually observance of the Law as interpreted by the scribes and Pharisees who sit on Moses' seat (23:2). It is from this conception that the promise to Peter is to be understood (16:17-19); Peter, the apostle of the circumcision, is the ideal leader and what he permitted or forbade should be the church's norm. Yet the full observance of this norm is rather a counsel of perfection than a binding precept. The ceremonial observances are after all "little" commandments in contrast to the "great" obligations of justice, mercy and faith (23:23) which are incumbent on all men. If these latter are observed, then salvation is not lost if "little" commandments are broken, or even if their breach is deliberately taught. But those responsible for such breaches will be "least" in the Kingdom; in contrast to the faithful Jewish Christians who sedulously observe not only the "great" but the "little" commandments as well (5:19). With this reservation the First Gospel eagerly approves and glorifies the Gentile mission. Nor did the reservation seem excessive; if Gentile believers are assured a place in the Kingdom, does it really matter whether this place is "high" or "low"?

It is not too far-fetched to find a similar conclusion taught in the obscure passage Revelation 14:1-5. Who are the 144,000 who are "not defiled with women, for they are virgins"? Contemporary interpreters generally explain this group as Christian ascetics; and if Revelation had been written a century or so later by a Hellenistic authors this explanation would seem almost axiomatic. But there is no evidence at all for so high an estimate on such asceticism before the close of the first century, particularly in the Jewish Christian circles from which Revelation comes. And the enormous number given to these assumed ascetics is incredible, even making all allowance for apocalyptic symbolism. What has not been sufficiently noticed is that this number is not new in the Book; it has appeared already in chapter 7 as the number of Jewish Christians, in contrast to the vastly great number of "ten thousand times ten thousand" from every nation, tribe, people and tongue. When this is recognized 14:1-5 offers no difficulty. Were not these Jewish believers the "first fruits to God and the Lamb"? Moreover in their mouth was never found the "lie" of confessing a false God before their conversion; and they have never been defiled by that worship of idols which the seer describes in the familiar Old Testament imagery of sexual license. So they have the preeminence; they know a song which they alone can sing and they "follow the Lamb whithersoever he goeth."

How was Paul regarded by Christians of this type? Matthew, past question, includes him among those who break the "little" commandments and teach men so to do; therefore destined to one of the "least" places in the Kingdom but not excluded from it; a mitigated approval but an approval none the less. The opinion of the writer of the Apocalypse may be gleaned from 21:14, where on the foundations of the City are written the names of the Twelve, giving them a unique and unrivalled authority; this is of course only what must be expected of so Jewish-Christian a work. But to find a covert attack on Paul in the condemnation of those who teach Christians to eat things sacrificed to idols (2:14, 20) is hypercritical. The adversaries here are gnostic (?) libertines, who also approve fornication. And eating things sacrificed to idols had taken on a new significance in the passionate struggle against emperor worship in which the church was now engaged.

It has not been sufficiently recognized that a corresponding attitude toward the superiority of Jewish Christianity pervades Luke-Acts. After all has been said about the Hellenism of the Third Gospel, it has fewer references to the Gentile mission than either Mark or Matthew; and it omits the word "Gospel" altogether. And in Acts the supreme Christian authority are the assembled "apostles and elders" in chapter 15, continued by their successors "James and the elders" in chapter 21. Luke, at the cost of some discontinuity, dislocates his sources and rearranges his material so that the beginning of the Gentile work in Antioch (11:19ff, which originally evidently followed 8:4) does not appear until a Palestinian precedent has been established by Peter in Caesarea and has been approved by the apostles in Jerusalem. Nor does the Paul of Acts rank with the Twelve. In neither of the accounts of his conversion in Acts 9 and 22 does Christ give him an apostolic commission (this appears however in 26:16 — by an oversight of Luke?) and the title "apostle" is bestowed on him — equally with Barnabas! — (14:4, 14) only after the ceremony in 13:1–3, which it is hard to read otherwise than as an ordination, making Paul actually an "apostle through men." Just so in the speech in Acts 13:31 he does not reckon himself among the witnesses of the resurrection, while in chapter 15 at the Council he appears only to bear witness and takes no part in the subsequent proceedings. The only mention of Paul's justification teaching is in the ambiguous verse 13:39 and "Gospel" appears in Acts only twice, once in Paul's mouth (20:24) and once in Peter's (15:7). Moreover the Paul of Acts is scrupulously Jewish in his own practices (15:18; 20:6, 16; 25:8; 28:17, etc.), fully justifying the praise of the Jerusalemites that "thou thyself walkest orderly, keeping the law" (21:24). In presenting this picture of Paul one purpose of Luke's, past doubt, was to reenforce his case against Roman persecution of Christianity by arguing that his religion was a variant form of Judaism and so entitled to the protection accorded to a *religio licita*. But it is very possible that Luke had likewise in mind Jewish Christian opposition to Paul and met it — with how good a conscience we know not — by simply denying its premises. Jewish Christians certainly never studied Paul's letters and knew about him only by repute; here in Acts was a portrait at which no one could protest.

On the other hand Paul certainly did not lack his disciples, who would defend their master's teaching with passionate zeal. The New Testament, however, contains nothing about their efforts during his lifetime and little in the decade or so following his death. The earliest pro-Pauline writing that we have is Mark's Gospel and this is pro-Pauline only in a secondary sense; it is not an outright effort to defend Paulinism but attempts to accomplish its purpose indirectly by its arrangement and presentation of traditional material about Jesus. Its polemical purpose is indicated none the less by its opening words, "The beginning of the Gospel of Jesus Christ." It has only been within comparatively recent years that the significance of these words has been understood; the term "Gospel" for an account of what Jesus said and did was so totally taken for granted that the phrase seemed obvious. But when Mark wrote the term had no such meaning; "Gospel" was a technical Pauline term and there is no evidence at all that the word was ever used technically by anyone else in the first two Christian generations. In Mark's day (*ca.* A.D. 70?) "The Gospel of Jesus Christ" would mean the presentation of Paul's message in terms of the teaching and work of Jesus; the corroboration of the Apostle by the Master. In presenting such a thesis Mark was, as has been said, hampered by the necessity of adhering to the tradition, which everyone knew so well that any radical departure would have been detected and rejected at once. Still, there was much that he could accomplish. A basic argument of Paul's opponents was the authority of the Twelve and this authority Mark sets out to discredit; over and over again he insists on Jesus' dissatisfaction with the disciples (4:13, 40; 6:52; 7:18; 8:17f; 9:19, 32, 34, 38; 10:14, 37, etc.) culminating in the final words of condemnation "they all left him and fled" (14:50). Nor is the picture of Peter, their leader, flattering. While he acknowledged the Messiahship, the sense he gave the title was so wrong and his own attitude so perverse that he was rebuked as nothing less evil than the climax of all evil,

"Satan" (8:33). The vision of the Transfiguration displays him equally without understanding (9:5). And in his last appearance the Gospel shows him in the ultimate extremity of weakness when he denies his Lord. Outside the Twelve the leaders of Jewish Christianity were the brethren of the Lord, whom Mark likewise depreciates. They attempt to interfere with Jesus, saying "He is beside himself," and are publicly disowned for their pains (3:21, 31–35). And Jesus declares that a prophet is not without honor save among his own kin and in his own house — and Mark leaves no doubt as to who these "kin" are by listing all four of the brothers by name (6:1–4).

By this condemnation of all the Christian leaders who could be cited as opposed to Paul, Mark clears the way for the Apostle's authority. For the more positive aspects of Paulinism, however, the Evangelist's lack of traditional material involves a more indirect approach. As regards the repeal of the Law he uses the elaborate section 7:1–23, whose moral — as he sees it — he brings out in v. 19 by an explicit note of his own, "making all things clean!" (contrast Mt. 15:20 where the deduction is limited strictly to the matter in hand). It is no accident that this declaration is followed by the scene with the Syrophoenician woman, the healing of the deaf mute in Decapolis and the second feeding of a multitude, this time on Gentile soil. But the primary thesis of Mark's Gospel is that Jesus was never a "Christ according to the flesh." His mission was to be fulfilled not on earth but from heaven; the Cross was no tragic mishap but from the first was inevitable; the means ordained by God by which the ransom of mankind was to be effected.

Of the other New Testament defenses of Paulinism the most familiar is Ephesians, which is so saturated with the Apostle's thought that it still finds able defenders as one of his genuine writings. The evidence however is against this; most notably when its author misunderstands the angelic "principalities and powers" of Colossians as the demoniac "spiritual hosts of wickedness in the heavenly places" (6:12). And Paul's hurried flow of thought, darting this way and that into all manner of irrelevancies, is replaced by an orderly and stately argument that proceeds without break from its premises to its conclusions. Nor is the treatment of the Law in 2:14–18 quite Pauline, for the "enmity" created by the Law is not primarily that between man and God but between Jew and Gentile; the wider context of the Epistle shows that while the "ceremonial" laws are indeed abolished, the "moral" laws remain eternal (6:2).

In John's Gospel, however, the mastery of Paulinism is complete; so complete that the language is no longer Pauline but Johannine. In certain matters, indeed, John goes beyond Paul. The latter tells us rapturously how his justification doctrine gives us peace with God; to John this peace is so complete that Paul's term "servant of God" is no longer appropriate: "no longer do I call you servants... I have called you friends" (15:15). To Paul again it was a matter of indifference whether a Christian chose to live as a Gentile or a Jew, provided no special divine sanction was claimed for either mode of life. But to John Jewish Christianity was virtual apostasy; the Lord's brethren are denounced as among those whom "the world cannot hate" (7:7). And to John the Jewish Law is a foreign thing; Christ in addressing Jews describes it as "your Law" (8:17; 10:34) and in speaking of Jews describes it as "their Law" (15:25). Whatever merit it may have had (10:35 — or is this verse an editor's gloss?), it contained no adequate revelation of God; even the Fourth Commandment stated an untruth in its attribution of "rest" to the Deity (5:17). But in John the Twelve are not associated with Jewish Christianity. Their failures to understand Christ are not used, as in Mark to depreciate them: their misunderstandings occur as part of the dialectic by which they are educated and their education reaches a triumphant conclusion (15:15f., 27; 17:18; 20:21, etc.). Here John simply assumes what all Christians of his day and of all later days assumed, that Christianity as he knew it was and must be the Christianity preached by the apostles. That their religion could have been defective or that they could have quarrelled among themselves was to him unthinkable.

John represents the final victory of Gentile over Jewish Christianity, which in the second century vanished as a force in Christianity as a whole. So to the Gentiles Paul's contention for their equality became an axiom, with, indeed, "equality" interpreted as "superiority." But acceptance of Paul's conclusion did not mean acceptance of the arguments he used to support it. On the contrary, his "faith, not works" antithesis and his dismissal of the entire Old Testament Law fell either on deaf ears or, worse, on the ears of gnostics who perverted Paul's teaching into pernicious nonsense.

The difficulty lay in the realm of practical teaching. To do simultaneous justice to all the aspects of Paul's — or John's — soteriology was an intellectual feat far beyond the abilities of the vast majority of Christians of their own and ensuing generations. The leaders of the early church were men of vast moral earnestness but by no means of corresponding speculative ability. And their people were largely very simple souls indeed, usually with minimal moral antecedents. For such men moral teaching was possible only in the most concrete terms of "Do this; Do not do that." And such terms are only incidental in the ethics of Paul, who, like Jesus, regards the act primarily in the terms of its motive. But analysis of acts into motives is not for beginners, who need rules in black and white.

In such rules the Old Testament abounds and the early non-Pauline missionaries to the Gentiles taught their converts these rules as a matter of course; and when these converts made other converts the same method was followed. It is fully exemplified by Clement of Rome, who gives a luxuriant variety of Old Testament citations for every duty he enjoins, almost completely ignoring both Jesus and Paul. Not that he depreciates Paul in the least, whom he upholds as the supreme exemplar of endurance (5:5–7); Clement has not the least suspicion that he in any way departs from the teaching of his hero, no more than he has when he cites Abraham and Rahab as exemplars of "faith *and hospitality*"! (10:7; 12:1 — noting that the former passage follows a direct citation of Rom. 4:3). Just so Barnabas doubtless thought himself a Paulinist as he allegorized away the Jewish ceremonial laws, although his allegory merely reestablishes these laws as binding moral precepts. The picture is clear enough; Paul had been canonized — but Paulinism was forgotten.

Yet even in the early second century the canonization was not everywhere accepted. A dissentient voice speaks in James, to whom the "faith, not works" antithesis is essentially immoral. Of course James did not understand Paul but we cannot doubt that he thought he did. To reconcile James and Paul used to belong to the ABC's of exegetical art; but men who write in the polemic style of James are not men who rejoice in seeing antitheses reconciled in an embracing synthesis.

With James, however, anti-Paulinism in the New Testament comes to an end. Despite all doubts the depth and beauty of the Epistles overcame all opposition. Two generations more and the Church was beginning an official affirmation of their inspiration; after two further generations to doubt Paul's infallibility was heresy. But the "Paul" whose "infallibility" was so dogmatically proclaimed was the Paul as interpreted at that day. Just as in Acts a Paul is described with whose teachings conservative Jewish Christians could not quarrel, just so in the second century a Paul was described with whose teachings the common Christianity was in complete agreement. Such is the Paul of the Pastoral Epistles.

In these writings the Old Testament no longer is a problem: "from a babe thou hast known the Scriptures which are able to make thee wise unto salvation through faith which is in Christ Jesus. Every Scripture is inspired of God, and profitable for teaching, for reproof, for correction" (2 Tim. 3:15f.). And the Law is no obstacle between God and man, far beyond man's abilities to fulfil. On the contrary the Law lays down rules of such obvious simplicity that every righteous man simply takes them for granted; it was enacted only to rebuke gross sinners (1 Tim. 1:8–11).

Real approximations to technical Pauline language occur — perhaps significantly — once and once only in each of the Pastorals (in 1 Tim. 1:13f.; 2 Tim. 1:9 and Titus 3:5). But in only the first of these does "faith" occur. The passage reads "I was before a blasphemer... howbeit... the grace of our Lord abounded exceedingly with faith and love." But even here "faith" by itself is deemed inadequate and is coupled with "love." And this same coupling occurs in the Pastorals seven other times, plus one occurrence of "faith and truth." Three times at least "faith" means only "fidelity"; thirteen times at least it means "orthodoxy"; while in the other seven instances it stands in some such conventional formula as that of 2 Timothy 3:15.

2 Timothy 1:9 is "Who saved us and called us with a holy calling, not according to our works, but according to his own purpose and grace." Titus 3:5 is "Not by works done in righteousness, which we did ourselves, but according to his mercy he saved us." Here without copying directly from the genuine Epistles the writer has constructed two perfectly Pauline sentences; even "grace" — the word destined to work confusion among exegetes — is used correctly. But the antithesis between "works" and "grace" is restricted

wholly to the pre-conversion state. Here the writer could rouse no dissent, for it was a Christian axiom that no man's earlier life, no matter how sinful, need bar him from reception. And it was likewise an axiom that far more converts were attracted from among sinners than from the wise and prudent. No one could maintain that God called men according to their works; the reason for His choice rests in His own inscrutable purpose.

But when the writer of the Pastorals describes how the call is made effectual, he continues the passage in Titus with "through the laver of regeneration and making us new through the Holy Spirit." These words in themselves are not un-Pauline, for even though Paul does not actually use the word "regeneration" to describe the effects of baptism, he certainly has the concept. Yet the verse as a whole Paul could never have written, for his basic tenet, "We are saved not by works but by faith" is converted into "we are saved not by works but by — *baptism*"! Not only is "faith" omitted from the verse in Titus altogether, but it is no accident that the Pastorals' only instance of "justify" as implied to sinners is in the following verse, describing the *post*-baptismal state. Though the soul believes never so ardently in Christ and in God's promises, there is no justification until baptism is received.

We are now in the stage of full ecclesiasticism. Baptism is no longer administered as soon as faith is professed; on the contrary a long period of testing and training is required in a catechumenate, which by the end of the second century might last three full years. Full and explicit faith was required before the catechumenate began, but in the eyes of the church this faith did not and could not justify; it was a necessary preparation for baptism but it was only a preparation. If a catechumen should die before he was baptized, confident hope of his salvation could be entertained only if his death was by martyrdom. And even in that case it was baptism, not faith, that saved, for martyrdom was reckoned as a true baptism, a "baptism of blood."

So once more, as has been said, Paul was canonized — and Paulinism was forgotten. Undoubtedly students of his letters were puzzled by passages, but the received opinion about such passages was voiced perfectly by the wholly orthodox and wholly pedestrian author of 2 Peter. Undoubtedly in the writings of beloved Paul there are things "hard to be understood," which "the ignorant and unsteadfast wrest ..., as they do the other Scriptures, unto their own destruction" (3:16). But since no Scripture is "of private interpretation" (1:20), these obscurities must have an explanation consonant with correct faith. Such an explanation exegetical art could always manage to find. And readers untrained in exegetical devices could simply pass over troublesome texts as beyond their understanding.

A VENTURE IN THE SOURCE ANALYSIS OF ACTS

MASSEY HAMILTON SHEPHERD, JR.
Episcopal Theological School

By the turn of the twentieth century intense interest in the critical play of source analyses of Acts definitely and suddenly began to wane. The general verdict, accepted by many who had indulged most strenuously in the game, was that nobody could win.[1] For over a generation now New Testament scholars have been reluctant to resume the fray. Conservatives have been content with the moderate analysis of Harnack since his criticism did not endanger their orthodox position concerning date and authorship of the book.[2] Those of more daring temper in criticism, such as the great Julius Wellhausen, confined their efforts to details without any overall attempt to assign, as did their nineteenth century predecessors, every verse or half-verse to a particular source and *Tendenz*.[3] The tentative application of form-criticism to Acts by Martin Dibelius has found surprisingly few followers.[4] The monumental com-

[1] Admirably summarized by A. Bludau, "Die Quellenscheidungen in der Apg.," *Biblische Zeitschrift* V (1907), 166-89, 258-81. See also the sound remarks of W. Heitmüller, "Die Quellenfrage in der Apostelgeschichte (1886-1898)," *Theologische Rundschau* II (1899), 47-59, and the change of mind of C. Clemen, *Die Apostelgeschichte im Lichte der neueren text-, quellen- und historisch-kritischen Forschungen* (Giessen, 1905).

[2] A. Harnack, *The Acts of the Apostles*, translated by J. R. Wilkinson (London, 1909).

[3] "Noten zur Apostelgeschichte," *Nachrichten von der königlichen Gesellschaft der Wissenschaften zu Göttingen*, Phil.-hist. Klasse, 1907, Heft 1, pp. 1-21; "Kritische Analyse der Apostelgeschichte," *Abhandlungen der königl. Ges. der Wiss. zu Göttingen*, Phil.-hist. Klasse, N.F. XV (1914) Nr. 2, pp. 1-56.

[4] "Stilkritisches zur Apostelgeschichte," ΕΥΧΑΡΙΣΤΗΡΙΟΝ, . . . *Hermann Gunkel*, ed. by H. Schmidt (Göttingen, 1923), 2. Teil, pp. 27-49.

mentary on Acts edited by F. J. Foakes Jackson and Kirsopp Lake takes a cautious position regarding the source problem and practically ignores the form-critical technique.[5] Though we must admit that the problem of sources used by the author of Acts will continue to defy any precise solution we cannot ignore being concerned with it. Upon its answer depends the evaluation of the trustworthiness of Acts as history, as over against its obvious and admitted purposes both kerugmatic and apologetic. Observation of the author's methods of composition in his gospel-volume affords warnings, but few clues to the critic regarding possible criteria of analysis. Two principles of our author's literary habit seem certain: 1) He uses sizeable blocks of his sources at a time, and follows them, in the main, in their order of contents.[6] 2) He so rewrites his sources that without them the critic is unable to recover them by detection of major differences in vocabulary and style. It may be said, too, that despite the author's freedom in revamping his material according to his own literary tastes, he does not play fast and loose with the written tradition before him; though he feels free to supplement it with items and emphases gathered out of oral tradition or correspondent to his own needs of interpretation.

See also S. E. Johnson, "A Proposed Form Critical Treatment of Acts," *Anglican Theological Review* XXI (1939), 22-31.

[5] See the article in Vol. II, pp. 121-204, of *The Beginnings of Christianity* (London, 1920-33), hereinafter cited as *BC*.

[6] There are exceptions, of course. The visit to Nazareth (Lk. 4:16 ff.) is certainly out of order (cf. vs. 23). But by putting it at the beginning of Jesus' ministry the author is able to use it as a key to the narrative which follows: the ultimate rejection of the gospel by the Jews. Similarly in the acts-volume the Pentecost story, as interpreted by the author, sets the stage for the story of the extension of Christianity from Jerusalem to Rome, from Judaism to the Gentile world. I have given reasons for believing that this pericope is also not in its original order as given in his sources in my article, "Paul and the Double Resurrection Tradition," *Journal of Biblical Literature* LXIV (1945), 237.

THE SOURCE ANALYSIS OF ACTS 93

The first of these principles is suggestive in respect to the much-debated chronology of Acts as over against the indications of time-sequence in the Pauline epistles. The disagreements between Acts and Paul will be then considered as due either to a faulty or misleading chronology in Acts' sources or to the author's habit of using his sources one at a time without harmonizing.[7] Only two dates in Acts can be secured by evidence external to the book itself: the death of Herod Agrippa I in the summer of 43 or spring of 44 A. D., and the proconsulship of Gallio in Achaia in 52 A. D.[8] A recent study of the famine under Claudius has fixed the year 46–47 as the most likely time in which Judaea was affected.[9] This date fits admirably with the chronology of Galatians, whether we interpret the second visit of Paul to Jerusalem to have been seventeen or fourteen years after his conversion. The crucifixion of Jesus occurred probably in the year 30, hardly any later.[10] There is no necessary reason to suppose that Paul's conversion did not occur within the year. But if one considers that to be compressing too closely the "born out of due time" of 1 Corinthians 15:8 then the fourteen rather than seventeen year interval between conversion and second visit may be adopted.

Acts is by no means irreconcilable with these dates. Paul's conversion occurred presumably after the martyrdom of Stephen; but there is no indication in Acts that any long

---

[7] The doublets which many critics detect in chapters 2–5 may illustrate this point. In the case of the Stephen story (6:8–15, 7:54–60) the author has probably not harmonized two sources, but reinterpreted an account of a lynching. See below.   [8] *BC*, V, 445 ff.

[9] K. S. Gapp, "The Universal Famine under Claudius," *Harvard Theological Review* XXVIII (1935), 258–65.

[10] See C. H. Kraeling, "Olmstead's Chronology of the Life of Jesus," *Anglican Theological Review* XXIV (1942), 335–37.

[11] I pass over here the view of some critics that the references to Paul's presence at Stephen's martyrdom are editorial additions (see, *e.g.*, Clemen, *op. cit.*, p. 30). They may well be so; but that does not prove that there is no historical basis for their insertion.

interval of time elapsed between the beginning of the Church and Stephen's death.[11] An enthusiastic, explosive movement such as primitive Christianity spreads rapidly and as quickly arouses opposition. "Hellenist" members probably belonged to the movement from the beginning.[12] The dating often given to Stephen's death of 36 A.D., the year following Pilate's recall, is much too late to fit any chronology of Paul's career. It assumes also that Stephen was not lynched but formally put to death by the Sanhedrin. This is very doubtful. As for the date of Aretas, it is unnecessary to wait until Tiberius' death to give him control of Damascus. Professor Lake has cleared this obstacle by pointing out that 2 Corinthians 11:32 f. does not suggest that Aretas was in control of Damascus at the time of Paul's escape, but the territory outside the city. His ethnarch was watching the city to catch Paul when he came out.[13] That Paul was beset at the same time by a Jewish plot within the city is perfectly possible.

The account in Acts of the famine relief mission of Paul and Barnabas is interrupted by the story of Herod Agrippa's persecution and death, which occurred "at that time," a vague reference to say the least. Actually the fulfilment of the mission is put by the author after the king's death. There is no reason why Agabus may not have prophesied the event and the Antioch church have begun its preparations for assistance before the king's death. A prophet may prophesy anything at any time. Modern critics notwithstanding, he does not have to wait until an event happens to prophesy it! But practically all critics who accept any sort of source analysis in Acts consider 12:1–23 as derived from a source other than 11:27–30, 12:25. Thus the two

[12] The Pentecost story implies this, but it is obviously "history with a purpose." Acts 6:1 is most indefinite as to time. But the references to Barnabas in 4:36-37, and to Mnason of Cyprus, "an original disciple," in 21:16 are revealing.

[13] BC, V, 193 f. This was also the view of Wellhausen.

passages need have no originally chronological connection. If the famine visit took place in 46–47, seventeen (or fourteen) years after Paul's conversion, it seems obvious that it is the same as the council visit of Acts 15. Most critics who are not ultra-conservative have long accepted this identification, and explained the double account in Acts of a "second visit" as due to the use of two sources. This solution raises at once the question of the chronology of the so-called first missionary journey of Paul. Did it occur before or after the conference in Jerusalem? Eduard Schwartz believed that it came after, in fact the first and second journeys were one and the same, and that the author has again probably misunderstood two traditions or sources of the same events.[14] This theory has recently been taken up again by Joachim Jeremias [15] and by Morton S. Enslin.[16] Such a theory accords perfectly with the literary habit of our author, mentioned above, of using his sources in fairly sizeable blocks and presenting their materials generally in the order in which he finds them.

A more radical solution of the question has of late been proposed by Professor John Knox. He would combine the two missionary journeys, as does Schwartz, but would place them before the second visit to Jerusalem.[17] The principal support for this thesis is an interpretation of 2 Corinthians 12:2 as a reference by Paul to his conversion

[14] "Zur Chronologie des Paulus," *Nachrichten von der königlichen Gesellschaft der Wissenschaften zu Göttingen*, Phil.-hist. Klasse, 1907, Heft 3, pp. 263–99.

[15] "Untersuchungen zum Quellenproblem der Apostelgeschichte," *Zeitschrift für die neutestamentliche Wissenschaft* XXXVI (1937), 205–21.

[16] "'Luke' and Paul," *Journal of the American Oriental Society* LVIII (1938), 81–91. K. Lake gave a hesitant consent in *BC*, V, 237 f.

[17] "'Fourteen Years Later': A Note on the Pauline Chronology," *Journal of Religion* XVI (1936), 341–49; "The Pauline Chronology," *Journal of Biblical Literature* LVIII (1939), 15–29. See also P. S. Minear, "The Jerusalem Fund and Pauline Chronology," *Anglican Theological Review* XXV (1943), 389–96.

"fourteen years ago." This exegesis is possible but it seems a bit forced. It requires one to adopt a fourteen rather than seventeen year interval between conversion and second visit. Again, this is a possible exegesis of Galatians 2:1, but it is not the most natural one. And Galatians 1:21 certainly implies that Paul had not extended his labors beyond the limits of Syria and Cilicia before the second visit. This is the view of Acts in its famine-visit source; and it is also implied in the address of the so-called apostolic decree in Acts 15:23.[18] One must admit with Knox that Acts cannot be harmonized with Paul. But Schwartz' chronology does more justice to the author of Acts and does not force the more natural meaning of the statements of the Pauline epistles.[19]

One suspects that Professor Knox has been led to his

[18] The decree may belong to the same source as the famine visit. Its historicity is another question. I cannot believe that it is an invention of the author in the same way as the speeches of Acts; for if it were one would expect him to include the churches of the "first" missionary journey in the address, particularly since the author viewed the decree as intended for those churches also (cf. 16:4). It has often been pointed out that Acts 21:25 (which comes from the "we-source") implies that Paul did not know of the decree until his final visit to Jerusalem. This seems to me unlikely. It is possible, indeed probable, that the decree forms no part of the decisions reached at the conference of Paul's second visit to Jerusalem. But I believe with Lietzmann that it underlies the dispute at Antioch (Gal. 2:11 ff.) and probably also the problem of table fellowship in the church at Corinth. See H. Lietzmann, "Der Sinn des Aposteldekretes und seine Textwandlung," *Amicitiae Corolla*, ed. by H. G. Wood (London, 1933), pp. 203-11.

[19] One point in Knox's chronology is indeed attractive — the questioning of Orosius' date of 49 for the edict of Claudius referred to in Acts 18:2. Without Orosius' explicit date one would infer from the Roman historians that it was 41. If Aquila and Priscilla came to Corinth in 41, and Paul arrived shortly thereafter, the Thessalonian letters would take on a new significance. Would not their apocalyptic element be related to the excitement caused in Jewry by Caligula's mad desire to set up his statue in the temple in Jerusalem — a project providentially prevented by his murder in January, 41? One must remember, however, that the Thessalonian church was predominantly Gentile, not Jewish (cf. 1 Thess. 1:19).

THE SOURCE ANALYSIS OF ACTS 97

solution by his dissatisfaction with fourteen "silent years," as he calls them, during which we know nothing of Paul's missionary activity in Syria and Cilicia. There are, of course, no letters of Paul extant to churches in these provinces; and his later zeal in collecting funds for the church in Jerusalem seems not to have been extended to these areas of his initial work. But the historian must content himself with the fact that there are many "silent" years in the history of primitive Christianity. What do we know of Paul's activities during his three years in Arabia, or during his last years after he reached Rome (even assuming that the imprisonment letters were written from Rome and not from Ephesus)? The materials for reconstructing a history of the Church from the death of Jesus until the death of Herod Agrippa I are extremely scanty. That the author of Acts has so presented these meagre bits as to fill almost half of his volume is no little evidence of his skill as a writer.[20] But it is the strenuous decade from Agrippa's death to Paul's final arrest that gives the historian his most connected and detailed account of a segment of the apostolic period, thanks to the letters of Paul and the diary-source of Acts. Indeed no other decade of the first century, unless it be the last, is as rich in primary material.

This last observation brings to the fore the problem of the literary relation, if any, between Acts and the letters of Paul. Professor Enslin has come to the view, by no means novel, that the author of Acts, a Pauline enthusiast, knew the letters by way of hearing, at least, but did not have a copy before him on the table when writing his history.[21] Most of the parallels in Acts which he cites come from the

[20] His method is one of double narratives and long speeches. Chapters 10:1–11:18 are a capital example. The view of C. J. Cadoux that the verse-summaries, such as 2:47b, 6:7, 9:31, etc., represent "quinquennial intervals" from the first Pentecost is fanciful; see "The Chronological Divisions of Acts," *The Journal of Theological Studies* XIX (1918), 333–41.

[21] *Op. cit.*; also in his *Christian Beginnings* (New York, 1938), p. 424.

Galatian and Corinthian correspondence. These letters contain, of course, the largest amount of biographical material. (In theology the author of Acts can hardly be described as a Paulinist.) Professor Knox has also given some circumstantial reasons why the author of Acts must have known the letters, reasons which are bound up with his post-Marcion date of Acts.[22] The Pauline corpus of letters was widely known by the end of the first century, from Antioch to Rome. If Acts was composed after that time it is difficult to imagine the author as totally ignorant of this correspondence. But it cannot be convincingly demonstrated that he used these letters as a "source." Professor Enslin admits as much by disclaiming the presence of a written copy of them in the hands of our author. The anti-Marcionist purposes of the author of Luke-Acts would, according to Professor Knox, be a sufficient deterrent from a studied use of the letters inasmuch as Marcion had made so much of them.

A better explanation is demanded, however, of the coincidence that the extant letters of Paul cover the same area, and perhaps time,[23] of missionary labors as is described in most detail in Acts. This fact is faced squarely and consistently in the hypothesis of Professor Edgar J. Goodspeed: the publication of Luke-Acts suggested to an Asian Paulinist, who knew Colossians and Philemon (= the letter from Laodicea), the location of other churches where letters of the apostle might be preserved. As a result of this search a corpus of Pauline letters was brought together and published, prefaced by the general letter which we know as "Ephesians." Only after this event did Paul become a

[22] J. Knox, *Marcion and the New Testament, An Essay in the Early History of the Canon* (Chicago, 1942), pp. 132–36.

[23] I leave aside a discussion of the question whether the imprisonment letters were written from Ephesus. I am inclined to believe that they were. If so, the coincidence of Acts and the letters is all the more striking.

literary influence.[24] By making Colossians-Philemon the nucleus of the collection – a point much strengthened by the affinity of Colossians and Ephesians – Professor Goodspeed meets beforehand any objection that a reading of Acts would not lead one to look for letters of Paul at Colosse and Laodicea. It might be said, however, that Acts does make Paul's Ephesian ministry a focus for extensive missionary propaganda throughout the province of Asia.[25]

The hypothesis of Professor Goodspeed regarding the origin of Ephesians and the collection of Paul's letters would not be disturbed if one were to posit not the publication of Luke-Acts in its final form as the occasion of the accumulation of the Pauline corpus but only the publication of that source of Acts underlying the latter part of the volume which is held together by the "we-passages." A "life of Paul" or, more properly, an *Acta Pauli*, recounting the mission work of the apostle from the time he set out from Antioch after the conference visit to Jerusalem until his arrival in Rome, would satisfy all the conditions of Professor Goodspeed's reconstruction of literary history. At the same time the data brought forward by Professor Enslin (or Professor Knox) could also be taken into account.[26] It is interesting that practically all the passages brought forward by Professor Enslin occur in places where one senses most strongly the hand of an editor or interpreter, and almost never in the context of the we-source.[27] If such a

[24] *The Meaning of Ephesians* (Chicago, 1933), pp. 4 ff.

[25] Cf. 19:10, 22, 26; 20:4.

[26] Knox has suggested this solution in these words: "The author of Luke-Acts may have had at hand for the construction of the Acts section not scattered sources merely but a unified work, or perhaps one work dealing with the early church in Palestine and Syria and another with Paul, which he merely altered and expanded. . . . This earlier work (or these earlier works) would antedate the publication of the letters of Paul." *Marcion and the New Testament*, p. 135.

[27] Only one such case is adduced by Enslin: Acts 20:3 and Romans 15:31. But this is hardly possible; the former refers to Jewish plots in Asia, the latter to Jewish plots in Judaea.

reconciliation of theories is correct, as I am inclined to believe, the date of the final composition of Luke-Acts is open to other considerations of criticism; the *terminus ad quem* does not have to be "Ephesians," which appeared most certainly in the early nineties of the first century.

Up to this point we have endeavored to show that a reasonable recognition of sources in Acts may solve the riddle of its relation to the Pauline letters, and in particular to the chronological discrepancies between Acts and these letters. It remains to attempt to define more closely what these sources are. Without desiring to claim any originality for my position, I should favor a three-source hypothesis: 1) A body of Judaean tradition centering around the figure of Peter. This is to be found in chapters 2–5, 9:32–11:18, 12:1–18, and parts of 15.[28] Much of this material is presented twice [29] and it is all very much reworked and reinterpreted by the final author. Whether this source came to him in oral or written form I should not wish to say; nor do I feel confident in or competent of passing judgment on whether it came to him in Aramaic or Greek. If it were a written source the author has freely excerpted and adapted such of it as served his more general purpose. The experience of glossolalia at Pentecost is the most obvious case of reinterpretation. The arrest of Peter and John by the temple authorities following the healing of the lame man at the Beautiful Gate is another. The charge against the apostles was the use of the Name of Jesus in exorcism (4:7); but the author makes the chief grievance the teaching of the people and proclaiming "in Jesus the resurrection of the dead." (4:2). The witness of the apostles to the resurrection is one of the main themes of our author. The Ananias and Sapphira story is linked with the "communism" of the early Jerusalem community; but this interpretation is also

[28] Possibly also 8:14–25.
[29] The imprisonments of chapters 4, 5 and 12, may be a triplet.

forced. The mission of Peter to Cornelius is full of reworking. As Dibelius has pointed out, the original kernel of the story is a tale concerning the power of the apostolic preaching. The author has transformed it so as to serve his interests in the admission of the Gentiles into the Church and the problem of table-fellowship raised thereby.[30] If there is any unity of theme binding this original Judaean source it is the miraculous power of the apostles — their "signs and wonders." For our author they are a means of rendering testimony to the resurrection (cf. 2:43 and 4:33).[31]

Our other two sources are extra-Palestinian, written, and Greek. I would identify them as: 2) A Hellenistic source emanating from Antioch, and 3) an *Acta Pauli* which we shall not hesitate to ascribe to "Luke." The latter is developed about the diary-notes, but it is not entirely an eyewitness account. And in addition to the speeches, the final author has doubtless added some independent stories gathered and reshaped from oral tradition. We have already stated our agreement with Schwartz that the "first" and "second" missionary journeys were historically one continuous mission. The Hellenistic source recounted the story up to the point of Paul's break with Barnabas over John Mark. (It is, of course, purely speculative whether this source contained further information as to Barnabas' missionary activities.) Luke's account of the initial stages of this mission was probably more summary and only clearly gets into its stride at 16:6. But I believe there are spurs of it in the "first" journey. Indeed it may well be that 13:13 is its first appearance. The sudden change from

[30] *Op. cit.*, pp. 38–39.
[31] It is possible that 10:1 ff. and 15:1 ff. are independent of this Judaean source. Note the uncommon use of "Simon" or "Symeon" as the name of Peter, and the fact that these two sections are "out of order," not a normal procedure of our author in using written sources.

"Barnabas and *Saul*" to "Those about *Paul*" and thereafter "*Paul* and Barnabas" (except 14:14) is impressive.³² It may be also that the peculiarly Pauline use of the term "apostle" found only in 14:4, 14, may be due to the Luke-source.³³ I should certainly assign the account of the circumcision of Timothy (16:1-3) to the Luke-source.³⁴

It is the Hellenist source which betrays the most marked peculiarities, setting it off at once from the Judaean source and from the Luke-source. (Some critics have denied the latter, especially those who accept the Western "we" reading in 11:28.³⁵) This is the history of the Antiocheans, the Cyprians and the Cyreneans, men led by "prophets and teachers," full of Holy Spirit and wisdom and faith. The source includes the Stephen and Philip stories of chapters 6-8, the Antioch traditions of 11:19-30, 12:24-13:12 (and beyond in the "first" journey), and probably also the conversion of "Saul." Its most characteristic term is "disciples," a word not used by Paul. In both the Judaean

---

³² One should be very cautious in using linguistic evidence as a criterion for source analysis in our author, but the use of ἀνάγειν (13:13) in the sense of "to sail" is very common in the "we-passages."

³³ Enslin believes these verses show acquaintance with 1 Cor. 9:16. But if the author had deduced this conception of an "apostle" from hearing this letter read, why was he not consistent in his use of the term throughout his book? For it is obvious that in the early chapters of Acts the term of apostle is applied only to the Twelve. It is more likely that our author found this use of the term in his source and left it unchanged. Perhaps he understood it as a description, not as a title. Note also that 14:2-3 is one of those "seams" which suggests a junction of sources.

³⁴ It is odd, to say the least, to find Paul circumcising Timothy at the same time our author attributes to him the dissemination of the apostolic decree. See note 18 above. The best explanation is that 16:4 is editorial, and the Luke-source contained no account or reference to the Jerusalem conference and its decisions. It began with the mission journey, starting from Antioch.

³⁵ Notably H. H. Wendt, "Die Hauptquelle der Apostelgeschichte," *Zeitschrift für die neutestamentliche Wissenschaft* XXIV (1925), 293-305. This reading belongs to the tradition that Luke was an Antiochene. It is noteworthy that the Chester Beatty papyrus does not contain this Western reading.

THE SOURCE ANALYSIS OF ACTS 103

and Lukan sources the Pauline "brethren" is preferred.[36] Other peculiarities of this Hellenist source in terminology are: "Hebrews" and "Hellenists" rather than "Jews" and "Greeks" (the more natural preference of our author), the "Twelve," as distinguished from the larger company of "apostles," and an exact use of the term "presbyter." R. Schütz tried to distinguish the source with reference to the variant Ἰερουσαλημ-Ἱεροσόλυμα, but one can only say that our source *probably* preferred Ἱεροσόλυμα.[37] Similarly little can be made of the variation "word of God" and "word of the Lord." They are so synonymous to our author that he uses them interchangeably.[38] I may, however, call attention to the use of εὐαγγελίζειν with the accusative of the thing as a linguistic peculiarity of our source.[39]

The Hellenist source is interested in persons rather than places, unlike the "diarist." Lists of names are given with identification marks, often of their native land (cf. 6:5, 13:1). The brief note about Barnabas in 4:36–37 is probably derived from this source.[40] And the list of the Twelve

---

[36] "Brethren" is used in 6:3 in a speech of the Twelve, and in 11:29 to describe the Judaean community. It also occurs in 15:22 ff. in connection with the apostolic decree (which I am inclined to assign to the Hellenist source); but here the Jerusalem community is speaking.

[37] *Apostel und Jünger, eine quellenkritische und geschichtliche Untersuchung über die Entstehung des Christentums* (Giessen, 1921).

[38] See W. Bousset, *Kyrios Christos* (Göttingen, 1926), pp. 221 f., n. 5.

[39] In 8:25 (an editorial passage) it takes an accusative of the place; in 16:10 ("we-passage") an accusative of the person. Instances of the use with accusative of the thing, outside our source are: 10:36 (an Old Testament quotation), 13:32 (in a speech), and 17:18 (where the Western text omits!).

[40] The misinterpretation of his name has often been remarked upon. The interpretation fits better the name of Menahem in 13:1. See *BC*, IV, 49. A. Loisy, *La Naissance du Christianisme* (Paris, 1933), pp. 157, 171, has questioned the historicity of Barnabas' original connection with the Jerusalem church, in the same way that many have sought to dissociate Paul from that community until his first visit to Jerusalem after his conversion. See note 11 above. One suspects the editorial hand of the final author in Acts 11:22–25.

in 1:13, as in Luke 6:14–16, may come from it also. It is not derived from Mark. The source is concerned with the Twelve as over against the Seven (6:1 ff.). I am inclined to include also the story of the selection of Matthias in our Hellenist source — though not necessarily the legend about Judas which is dovetailed into the pericope.[41] Interest in appointment or ordination to office is characteristic of this Antioch material (cf. 6:6, 13:3, 14:23). The heroes of this old tale of Hellenistic Christianity are the prophets. Stephen and Philip are certainly not "deacons" in the later ecclesiastical sense, but ecstatics and visionaries (cf. 6:8, 15; 7:55; 8:26, 39). The coming of Agabus to Antioch with his dire prophecy made a great impression.[42] Barnabas and Saul are listed among the "prophets" (13:1). The apostle has himself witnessed to his own gifts as an ecstatic (1 Cor. 14:18). One other characteristic of the Hellenist source is worthy of note — its disregard of precise indications of time. In this respect it contrasts very noticeably with the source which follows it, what we have called Lukan. Only in 11:26 is a definite period given.[43]

The Hellenist source gives us our best insight into the dynamic, propulsive and unpredictable character of primitive Christianity. It presents the ready adaptation of the move-

[41] I should be certain of it if the Western reading μαθητῶν in 1:15 is correct.

[42] When Agabus reappears in the "we-passages" (21:10) he is introduced anew as though we had not read of him before. Does this not suggest a different source?

[43] It seems to me that the evidence of chronological data set forth by Harnack, *op. cit.*, pp. 1 ff., contradicts his own interpretation of it. Even in the passages of the Luke-source which are not eye-witness accounts there is a great deal more precision in dating, such as 17:2, 18:11, 19:8, 19:10, 20:3, 20:31. It is perhaps quibbling to ask whether or not the dating of 11:26 really belongs to the Hellenist rather than to the Lukan material. 15:35–36 is more in the manner of the Hellenist source. When we recall that the two sources are confused by the author because of his making an extra visit of Paul to Jerusalem, the shifting of chronological notes does not seem impossible.

THE SOURCE ANALYSIS OF ACTS

ment to 'all sorts and conditions of men.' There are no racial animosities, no marked anti-Jewish feelings. It is not apologetic. It accepts without argument the universal implications of the faith, the uncontrollable working of the Spirit in all times and places. By contrast the Lucan source, more unified by a single dominant personality, has a larger sense of inevitable destiny, of a specific directing of the Spirit toward a particular line of march of the gospel message. Full of tension between Jew and Gentile it builds up to a climactic clash of opposing forces in which the fate of the hero is ultimately determined. It is true, the final author of Acts may have lent to this drama a simplification and concentration which add to the intensity of the growing conflict.

The consummate art of the final author, however, is the skill with which he has welded his sources into a unity of theme larger in perspective than any of them. This theme he never loses sight of from its initial announcement: "you shall receive power when the Holy Spirit comes upon you, and you shall be my witnesses in Jerusalem and in all Judaea and Samaria and unto the ends of the earth." Through all the troubles and vicissitudes of external opposition and internal conflict the promise is fulfilled with Paul at Rome, "preaching the kingdom of God and teaching the things concerning the Lord Jesus Christ with all boldness and *without hindrance*." However easy it might be to cavil at details of historical inaccuracy, to be disappointed at the meagreness of source material for so large an undertaking, one cannot but be impressed by the author's depth of insight into the meaning of his historical subject, an insight which in its concluding utterance is truly prophetic.

A SUBSIDIARY MOTIVE FOR THE WRITING OF THE DIDACHE

SHERMAN ELBRIDGE JOHNSON
Episcopal Theological School

"The riddle of the Didache," as Vokes called it,[1] has not been completely solved. Nor should we expect, in the present state of our knowledge, to arrive at a solution with which everyone will agree. For that which makes it a riddle is also that which renders it important: it obviously contains some historical material of great value which is difficult to fit into ready-made categories. Like every really important discovery, it tends to raise as many problems as it solves; and, since the Didache affects our ideas of the development of the eucharistic liturgy, the literary relations of other documents, and the origin of the ministry, one can say that scarcely any find of the nineteenth century has been more upsetting and stimulating for the study of Christian origins.[2]

Opinion seems gradually to be settling on a late date for the document which Bryennios discovered. Muilenburg held that it is in literary dependence upon Barnabas and Hermas and so is later than both.[3] The most recent treatment of its literary relationships, that of Goodspeed, derives the Didache from the Greek original of the ·Latin Doctrina. The latter writing was composed early in the second century.[4] Even if one accepts (as I do) the judg-

[1] F. E. Vokes, *The Riddle of the Didache* (London, 1938).
[2] It is the Didache which rendered both the traditional Catholic and Presbyterian theories of ministerial origins untenable, and demanded such new reconstructions as those of Sohm and Streeter.
[3] J. Muilenburg, *The Literary Relations of the Epistle of Barnabas and the Teaching of the Twelve Apostles* (Marburg, 1929).
[4] E. J. Goodspeed, "The Didache, Barnabas and the Doctrina," *Anglican Theological Review* XXVII (1945), 228–247.

ment of Wilson that the earlier parts of Hermas are to be dated in the neighborhood of 100 A.D.,[5] the Didache is probably not earlier than 150 and may be as late as 175. For, as we shall see, the author uses more than one of our gospels and regards them as Holy Scripture; and, while the presence of prophets lends the book an illusion of antiquity,[6] the prophets themselves are carefully controlled by ecclesiastical custom and precept.

Whether the Didache is Catholic, or, as Vokes thinks, Montanist, is not very important. If it is the latter, it is a strange species of Montanism which in nearly all respects approximates the position, spirit, and methods of the Catholic Church. It is more important to ask what function it might have fulfilled in the church for which it was written. If we can get a satisfactory answer to this question before trying to decide what it teaches us about the origins of the ministry, we may be saved from some of the perils of circular reasoning.

First of all, it is a catechetical manual. No matter how archaizing it may be, the author intends that chapters 1–6 shall be taught to converts. While most of the remaining sections are addressed to those in authority, their content would be of interest and value to the catechumen, and the final section rounds out the book by the promise made to the faithful of the return of Christ.

But it is also a manual of procedure for a matured church. It tells how to baptize and to celebrate the eucharist, how to recognize the true prophet from the false, what kind of men should be appointed bishops and deacons, and it gives standards of teaching (11:1 f.) and simple rules for discipline (15:3 f.). At the same time, it fails to set up a norm for Christology or to prescribe any formula for ordination. Χειροτονήσατε in 15:1 may mean no more than

[5] W. J. Wilson, "The Career of the Prophet Hermas," *Harvard Theological Review* XX (1927), 21–62.   [6] Vokes, *op. cit.*, p. 117

"appoint." While the author wishes to preserve (or revive!) prophecy, and the prophets are allowed considerable liberty in eucharistic prayer (10:7), teaching, and symbolic action (11:1), the phenomenon is carefully controlled. Once his status as a true prophet is unquestionably determined, it is an unforgivable sin to put him to the test (11:7), but the Church's tradition has previously set up definite criteria for recognizing the prophet. The tests by which a Proteus Peregrinus may be screened out (11:4–6, 12) are no doubt useful; but what is more significant is that the apostles and prophets are to be treated according to the ordinance *of the gospel* (11:3), and that the standard by which the true prophet is known (*i.e.* chapters 1–10) is full of *synoptic teaching authoritatively expounded*. No longer is it possible for the Pneuma to blow completely as it will. A prophet (or perhaps we should call him a teacher) like the author of the Epistle of Barnabas had far more scope.[7] Unembarrassed by the control of the gospels, he romped through the Old Testament, finding there the prophecy of Christ, and the prediction of freedom from that Law which he believed the Jews had perversely misunderstood.[8] His religion was no doubt lopsided from the point of view of the Didache (just as Hermas' was); he had much to say about morality, baptism, and the Cross, but made no reference to the eucharist. The earlier prophets and teachers were more like Barnabas; they might have little contact with the gospel tradition, and depend instead on the Old Testament, their own inspiration, and the prevailing faith in the heavenly Lord; the Didache wished them to keep their freedom, but within some definite bounds. Not that the Didache is anti-prophetic — that would be an absurd paradox — it simply belongs to a later age.

[7] See Barn. 9:9, "He who has placed in our hearts the implanted gift of his teaching knows."
[8] The Didache likewise rejects the ceremonial law.

The thesis of this article is that there is a third motive for the writing of the expanded Didache. While it is a subsidiary one, it is none the less real and important, and it throws light on second century Christianity. The author or compiler wished to deal with certain matters which were already covered in the gospels, notably ethical instruction, the signs of Christ's return, the importance of conversion and steadfast discipleship, and the necessity of accepting those whom Jesus sends to proclaim his message. Often the gospels were obscure, and Jesus' demands, on the face of them, seemed contrary to common sense. But he needed to go further: any number of topics, touched upon by the gospels and other Christian writings, needed explanation and amplification.

On the other hand, while the already existing short Didache (or Two Ways, if one prefers that term) was a useful manual for converts, it obviously had little connection with the gospel tradition. The older writing was often close to the ethical spirit of Christ: "You must not hate any man; some you must love more than your life. . . . Do not be angry, for anger leads to murder;" and at the very outset it coupled love of God and neighbor, as Jesus had done. But if it was now to be used in churches which read and valued the written gospels, surely it ought to contain gospel teaching.

I

One may ask why the author chose the literary form which he did, if the Didache is, among other things, a commentary on the gospels and other Christian books. To write "Notes on the Gospels," as a modern would do, was out of the question. A commentary would never claim the authority which the writer believed his interpretation had. For he had "the mind of Christ"; his explanations were simply the drawing out of the meaning which the Lord him-

THE WRITING OF THE DIDACHE

self had intended. And, furthermore, the earliest commentaries were written by heretics.

A first century Christian might have met the need by composing a new gospel. That is what Matthew did; his explanations of the obscurities of earlier sources are apparent on nearly every page. John, in a still more radical fashion, set forth "the Eternal Word in the Modern World," [9] dealing with all kinds of contemporary doctrinal issues. Mark is no exception to the rule; he carefully draws out what he takes to be the true meaning of the parable of the Sower. There is abundant material in the four gospels for the study of early Christian methods of interpretation.

But our second century author could not adopt the gospel form. For one thing, he apparently felt no need for writing the entire story of Jesus. He does not have the burning interest in the Cross which the Apostle Paul and the author of Barnabas exhibited. Perhaps the fact of the Risen Christ alive among his people was sufficient for him; it is not redemption and forgiveness through Christ's sacrifice for which he thanks the Father, but life, knowledge, faith, immortality, spiritual food and drink, and eternal light which come through Jesus the παῖς.[10] What the Didachist needed for his church was a book more like the hypothetical Q document, which (after a section on John the Baptist) began with the start of Jesus' ministry and the Great Sermon and concluded with an apocalyptic section.[11] But even Q (which had probably disappeared long since) contained more material than he required.

There was a second and decisive reason for not writing

[9] The title of a book by B. S. Easton and H. C. Robbins (New York, 1937).

[10] Cf. Acts 2:24; Lk. 24:26, where no atonement ideas are expressed. See also A. D. Nock, in A. E. J. Rawlinson, ed., *Essays on the Trinity and the Incarnation* (London, 1928), p. 96, *n*.

[11] So the reconstructions of Harnack, Wendt, Hawkins, Streeter, F. C. Grant, and others; Bacon, however, thought Q (S) was a complete gospel.

a gospel: it would not have been accepted as authentic. The Fourth Gospel, which had long existed, had a difficult enough time winning its way, and, if R. M. Grant is right, its position was still insecure in the year 175.[12] The date does not greatly matter; the point to note is that the Didache does not quote John and has only a few phrases which remind one of the gospel's language. In all probability, John was not yet accepted everywhere as canonical, and a fifth orthodox gospel would have still less opportunity.

The author of the Didache may, indeed, have thought it improper for him to write a gospel. He had great reverence for Matthew, which for him was *the gospel*; the term is used, as in Justin Martyr, to refer to a book. The Lord commands use of the Lord's Prayer in its Matthaean form "in his Gospel" (8:2; cf. 11:3 and especially 15:3 f., where the rule in Mt. 18 for settling church disputes is alluded to). Didache 3:2 f. follows Matthew's order (5:21 f., 25 f., 27) in listing the vices. In 2:2 f. the commandments are quoted from Matthew, not Mark or the LXX, though the Latin Doctrina has them in the order of Deut. 5:17 f., LXX.[13] The Matthaean doctrine of two moral standards, one for the ordinary Christian and one for the perfect, dominates the Didache (1:4=Mt. 5:39, 48), and is applied to teachings other than those drawn from Matthew, *e.g.* 6:2. While the author made some use of Luke (and Acts), Matthew was his favorite, and he probably had no desire to detract from the popularity of this complete and impressive gospel.[14]

---

[12] R. M. Grant, "The Fourth Gospel and the Church," *Harvard Theological Review* XXXV (1942), 95–116.

[13] Cf. S. E. Johnson, "The Biblical Quotations in Matthew," *ibid.* XXXVI (1943), 150 f.

[14] Matthew and Luke are woven together in several places, *e.g.* 1:3 f., 5; 16:1. The simplest explanation is that the author is thoroughly acquainted with both gospels and is quoting from memory. These two gospels must often have been conflated in the second century; see, *e.g.*, the gospel material in 2 Clem., the Protevangelium of James, the fragments of the Gospel of the Ebionites, and the list of apostles in the Epistle of

II

Another, and very ingenious, form was therefore chosen. The new book claimed the authority, not of a lesser figure like Luke or Mark, or of a single apostle, but of all twelve. Had the Didache rested its claim on a single apostle, it could easily have been rejected as a pseudepigraph. It gained further verisimilitude because, unlike the Epistle of the Apostles, which made a similar claim, it did not attempt the hazardous business of gospel narrative. It was simply an instruction of Christ to his principal disciples, laying down the terms on which Gentiles were to be converted, making arrangements for church life, and explaining obscurities in his previous teaching. Perhaps, as Professor A. D. Nock has suggested to me, the author thought of the Risen Christ as addressing the Twelve during the forty days before the Ascension,[15] further explaining his command that they should be witnesses and should proclaim repentance and remission of sins to all nations (Lk. 24:47 f.; Acts 1:8).

This use of the Twelve as the guarantors of church tradition is itself a mark of late date. Matthew had much to do with establishing the "twelve disciples," as he called them, in this place of authority, and so did Luke-Acts and the Book of Revelation. And as the Church went through a time of testing — particularly from Marcion's day on — the Twelve were increasingly appealed to by the orthodox. One sees this in the canonization of the Book of Acts and

---

the Apostles. Matthew was the most popular gospel, as everyone knows. It is the basis of all the early apocryphal gospels except Ev. Aegypt., and it dominates the Protevangelium of James, the Epistle of the Apostles, and the Ascension of Isaiah. It was the gospel of Ignatius of Antioch. Luke and John are conflated in P. Egerton 2 and elsewhere; cf. R. M. Grant, *op. cit.*, 98 f. See also note 22 below.

[15] As in the Epistle of the Apostles, the longer ending of Mark, and perhaps the Preaching of Peter (Clem. Al. *Strom.* vi. 5. 43).

in the composition of the Preaching of Peter and the Epistle of the Apostles.[16] The Twelve are the Didache's heroes, not Paul. The Didache is not necessarily anti-Pauline, but it is certainly non-Pauline. Indeed one would expect that a book which is so akin in spirit to Matthew's gospel would have this character. While there are echoes of Pauline language here and there, Barnett is unable to find a single clear case of quotation from the Pauline letters.[17] As we have seen, the preaching of the Cross is omitted, though it was prominent in Barnabas.[18] The eucharistic prayers make no reference to it or to the Last Supper. Vokes says of the detailed instructions for baptism in chapter 7, "All this is due to a desire to find in the New Testament as much as possible about baptism, and then to expand it as much as possible" (p. 118). Why then does not the Didache bring more New Testament passages to bear on eucharistic practice? Perhaps the tradition with which the author was familiar did not mention the Last Supper in its eucharistic prayers. Does this in itself indicate a neglect of Paul? [19] There is, moreover, at least one place where the Didache is in clear opposition to Pauline ideas: "As for food, bear what [yoke] you can, but keep strictly from idolatrous meat, for it is worship of dead gods" (6:3). This sounds

[16] Note also Gospel of Peter 14:59, "We the twelve disciples of the Lord," and the way in which the Muratorian fragment places the authority of the Twelve behind the Fourth Gospel. Cf. also J. Knox, *Marcion and the New Testament* (Chicago, 1942), pp. 119 f., 135 f.; E. J. Goodspeed, *The Formation of the New Testament* (Chicago, 1926), p. 75; also W. Telfer, "The *Didache* and the Apostolic Synod of Antioch," *Journal of Theological Studies* XL (1939) 133-46, 258-71, an article called to my attention after this essay was written.

[17] A. E. Barnett, *Paul Becomes a Literary Influence* (Chicago, 1941), pp. 207-212.

[18] The σημεῖον ἐκπετάσεως is an apparent exception, but in any case it does not indicate that Christ suffered to redeem men from sin.

[19] It may also indicate that the tradition goes back to the apostolic age. Professor Nock has remarked to me that if the author used older sources in chapters 1-6, as we know that he did, he may have had other old sources for the rest of the book. The Didache is an ingenious compilation of many materials.

THE WRITING OF THE DIDACHE 115

like an utterance of the "weak," *i.e.* strict party, as Paul calls it. The moral standard perhaps demands vegetarianism (cf. Rom. 14:1 f.), or it may be keeping of the so-called Apostolic decree; and the Pauline principle of "asking no scrupulous questions" (1 Cor. 10:27) is completely ignored. If the author knows Paul, he regards his teaching as too liberal for safety. Other passages, while not anti-Pauline, are non-Pauline. 2:5 reflects the emphasis of Matthew (and Jesus) on deeds, not words. 4:6, "If you have acquired anything by your hands, you shall give a ransom for your sins," is particularly remarkable in view of the absence of any preaching of the Cross. These two passages, found also in the older Didache, probably are in complete harmony with the spirit of the church for which the Didachist wrote. 11:7 forbids any testing or discerning of spirits, whereas in 1 Cor. 12:10 (cf. 14:29) this activity itself is a gift of the Spirit.

III

The most characteristic trait of the Didache as a gospel commentary is that it attempts to put the sayings of Jesus on a rational, "common sense," basis as much as possible. Many of Jesus' commandments are vivid, hyperbolical, prophetic. They prick the conscience of those who face them squarely, and call forth heroic response. Matthew, while he reproduced his tradition with considerable fidelity, had already speeded up the process of adjusting them to a more sober and less enthusiastic church life (*e.g.* Mt. 19:11 f., 21). To the second century church it was axiomatic that Jesus' sayings must be practicable.[20] He might well make

[20] One observes the "common sense" tendency in the apocryphal logion quoted by Eusebius *Theoph.*, E. Preuschen, *Antilegomena*[2] (Giessen, 1905), p. 7; E. Hennecke, *Neutestamentliche Apokryphen*[2] (Tübingen, 1924), p. 31; in *Clem. Hom.* iii. 5; and Ep. of App. 40. Cf. S. E. Johnson, "Stray Pieces of Early Christian Writing," *Journal of Near Eastern Studies* V (1946), 40–54.

stringent demands on a few followers whose moral strength and resolution were great, they would reason; but for the rank and file he must have planned an ethic suitable to their abilities.[21] The Didache quotes "Love those who hate you" (1:3), but in the same verse the command to love one's enemies becomes "Pray for your enemies." [22] It is easier to do this, and to fast on behalf of persecutors, than actually to love them. However, if a man can love those who hate him, he will have no enemy. Just as in Romans 12:20 f., the expectation is that obedience to the law of Christ will produce desirable results.[23] Another passage dealing with love and hate (2:7) departs from the Sermon on the Mount in the interest of different treatment for different groups. Knopf remarks: "The love of enemies which Jesus demands has shrunk to a prayer for unbelievers that they may be converted: the heart belongs only to brothers in the community." [24] Similarly the author could not conceive of evil thoughts as on the same plane with overt action. He had to explain carefully that pride and

---

[21] K. E. Kirk, *The Vision of God* [2] (London, 1932), Lecture III.

[22] Vokes, *op. cit.*, p. 63 f., notes that the passage is similar to Justin *Apol.* i. 14. 3. He says: "It cannot be by chance that both Justin and the Didache take the 'love' from before 'your enemies' and replace it by 'pray for.' . . . These peculiarities of the Didache in its conflation of Matthew and Luke seem to be due to the influence of Justin." Dr. Bruce M. Metzger of Princeton Theological Seminary also calls to my attention the fact that several scholars have noted a similarity between Didache 1:4 and Tatian's *Diatessaron*; see, *e.g.*, A. Harnack, *Die Lehre der zwölf Apostel* ("Texte und Untersuchungen," II, Leipzig, 1886), 78 f.; Th. Zahn, *Geschichte des neutestamentlichen Kanons* (Erlangen, 1888), I, 930–32; J. R. Harris, *The Teaching of the Apostles* (Baltimore, 1887), p. 98. The parallel is not so close that much weight can be placed on it. It is, furthermore, interesting to note that the Way of Life begins in 1:2 with a Jewish moral standard, the Summary of the Law combined with the negative Golden Rule, and then uses the teaching of Jesus as a kind of talmud or commentary on it.

[23] Cf. J. Weiss, *Paul and Jesus* (London, 1909), p. 126 f.

[24] *Die apostolischen Väter* (Handbuch zum N. T., Ergänzungs-Band, Tübingen, 1920), *ad loc.*

anger *lead* to murder (cf. Jas. 4:1 f.) and that lust *leads* to fornication (3:2 f.). These last two passages were in the foundation document, but they fitted in completely with the compiler's point of view and he would have seen no reason for changing them.

The Christian must not resist one who takes his property away, and, if the Greek text is correct, the Didache says that he may as well acquiesce with good grace, for he will be unable to protect himself (1:4).[25] In the next verse a homiletical statement is tacked on to the command "Give to everyone who asks you." Furthermore, the generous one is protected by stern warnings against taking alms unless they are actually needed. The curse in 1:5b is drawn from Matthew 5:26, and the author is thus able to make use of the "adversary" saying, which must otherwise have been completely obscure to him. Finally he adds from an unknown source, "Let your alms sweat into your hands until you know to whom you give." The warm "Franciscan" generosity of the gospel has at last been completely domesticated.

Apparently the economic problem is serious enough, and members of the church cannot afford to waste their property.[26] A travelling apostle had to be received as the Lord (11:4, cf. Mt. 10:40) and a prophet must be given hospitality (Mt. 10:41), but the Lord had ordained no money gifts for his heralds, only food for their immediate hunger (Mt. 10:9-11), and one who asks more is an impostor (11:5 f.). Other attempts are made to define just who is sent by

---

[25] This sounds almost like Epictetus. K. Lake, *The Apostolic Fathers* (London, 1919), I, 311, accepts Harnack's conjecture καίπερ δυνάμενος. Knopf, however, *ad loc.*, takes the phrase as referring to the inward disposition of the "perfect"; it is internally impossible for him to protect his own by force or to go to court about it.

[26] Cf. Acts of John Lat. XVI, in M. R. James, *The Apocryphal New Testament* (Oxford, 1924), p. 257 f.; also the moralizing additions in Lk. 16:11 f.

Jesus and therefore is to be received as the Lord himself: he must teach in accordance with the Didache (11:1), and even after he is received he must be tested (12:1).

Several other curious exegetical twists can be observed. When Matthew recorded the sayings about the fasts of the hypocrites (6:16), he no doubt thought of the hypocrites as including all the members of the synagogue, not merely the Pharisees. The Didache makes this explicit and points out that they even fast on the wrong days (8:1). Likewise, what is wrong with the hypocrites' prayer is not that it is insincere, ostentatious, or needlessly prolix (Mt. 6:5–8); it is simply that it is Jewish (8:2). Yet the Christian, like the Jew, is to pray three times a day (8:3).

In another passage, the teaching of the Sermon on the Mount is applied to the cultus. The "dogs" of Matthew 7:6 are the unbaptized, and one must not give them the holy food of the eucharist (9:5).[27] What could be more natural? It was almost the only "holy thing" known to the second century Christian.

Two other interpretations are completely understandable. "Hosanna to the son of David" (Mt. 21:9) becomes "God of David" (10:6). The unforgivable sin against the Holy Spirit (Mt. 12:31), which in every age terrifies the simple, is explained as the testing or discerning of him who speaks in the Spirit. And why not? Was not this the most striking manifestation of the Spirit which the early church knew?

Matthew's eschatological ideas, particularly his doom chapter, made a profound impression on the author. Those who lead the Church astray (Mt. 24:4) teach things contrary to the moral sections of the Didache (6:1). But when the end comes the Church will be gathered into the Kingdom from the four winds (Mt. 24:31; Did. 10:5). The

[27] Cf. *Clem. Hom.* iii. 5; *Rec.* ii. 3; Hennecke, *op. cit.*, p. 46.

THE WRITING OF THE DIDACHE

last chapter of the Didache is, in fact, largely built up out of Matthew 24. One who read Matthew and Luke carefully would, of course, notice that the last great section of Jesus' public teaching was a discourse on the end of the age, and there could be no more logical climax for a *didache*. One need not suppose that the Didache is written at a time of unusual tension. At almost any period in church life a teacher may feel that there are too many false prophets abroad, that "the love of many has grown cold," and that the people need a little apocalyptic reawakening. The presence of this chapter merely indicates that Matthew 24 stood in need of further explanation. It is used in such a way as to urge the people, not merely to moral effort, but to greater regularity in church attendance (16:2; cf. Heb. 10:25). The Antichrist is introduced into Matthew's scheme in language that suggests 2 Thessalonians 2:9. Even the curse which oppresses the people (perhaps persecution, even martyrdom) will be a means for their salvation. The last events are schematized and care is taken to assert that not all the dead are raised.[28] And, above all, the author deals with the great exegetical problem in Matthew 24:30 — what was the sign of the Son of Man? Though he answers in cryptic language — as is quite fitting in an apocalypse — he has a clear idea in his mind. His σημεῖον ἐκπετάσεως is the appearance of the Son of Man on the Cross with outstretched hands. This is proved not only by the ἐξεπέτασα in the parallel passage in Barnabas 12:2–5, but also by the fact that in the Gospel of Peter 10:39 the Lord's Cross follows him into heaven and in the Epistle of the Apostles 16 (cf. also Ethiopic text of the Apoc. of Peter) it will go before him when he returns.[29]

---

[28] Cf. the mention of the last judgment also in Barnabas 21.
[29] Cf. my article, *JNES* V (1946), 51 f.; Muilenburg, *op. cit.*, p. 80; Knopf *ad loc.*; also Jn. 12:32, "I, if I be lifted up, will draw all men unto myself."

IV

The other principal trait of the Didache as a commentary is that it continually gives further directions for actions commanded in the New Testament books. Vokes sees in this an antiquarian interest in the New Testament. A simpler explanation, however, is that now the gospels were coming to be regarded as a canon of scripture; and whereas previously the various rites had been carried on according to existing tradition, it was now natural that people should ask what these authoritative books had to say about Christian practice. Had the Lord made sufficient provision for what he had commanded? The answer could be found in the gospels as interpreted by the Didache.

An early Christian might well ask what formula should be used in baptism, since Acts speaks of "baptism in the name of the Lord Jesus." But to be baptized in the "name of the Lord" (Did. 9:5) is to have received the trinitarian formula (7:1, 3). Questions of the necessity of running water (presupposed in some passages of Acts), and of immersion (the obvious New Testament custom), would have arisen. And what preparation should the baptizer and the candidate make (chapter 7)? Coupled with baptism was the eucharist, which Jesus had commanded in the gospels without telling how it was to be celebrated. It was also necessary to find dominical authority for confining the sacred meal to the baptized (9:5) and desirable to base the custom of a Sunday eucharist on something besides universal custom (14:1). This offered a splendid opportunity to apply to the eucharist the gospel provision that a man must be reconciled to his brother before offering his gift at the altar (14:2; cf. Mt. 5:23 f.; Ign. *Trall.* 8:2). What other sacrifice could Jesus have had in mind, since the Jewish sacrifices were abolished? Pagan sacrifices were to dead gods

(6:3). The only pure sacrifice possible among the Gentiles was prayer, in this case the eucharistic prayer (14:3; cf. Mal. 1:11, 14).

Fasting, prayer, and almsgiving likewise called for some attention. They must be in accordance with the "gospel of our Lord" (15:4; no doubt the reference is to Mt. 6:1–18). A time will come when the bridegroom will be taken away (Mt. 9:15), and then what arrangement should be made for fasting? Obviously not when the hypocrites fast, but on other days (8:1). And, whereas the hypocrites recite the *Shema'* at regular hours, the Christian must thrice daily offer the prayer commanded by the Lord in his gospel (8:2 f.).

There is also a simple rule for discipline, drawn no doubt from Matthew 18:15–35. The one who wrongs his brother is to be "sent to Coventry" until he repents (15:3).

Apostles and prophets appear to be coupled together in Matthew 10:40 f., hence they must be taken up in Didache 11:3–12. Vokes points out that the apostle is disposed of briefly and more attention is devoted to the prophet. But it is not necessary to see Montanism in this, for prophets are known in orthodox circles as late as the third century. The qualifications of an apostle were well known, and the apostles were dead; hence only the briefest explanation of the gospel ordinance was needed (11:4–6). It is the prophet who is a contemporary figure and needs to be discerned for what he is (11:7–12, perhaps also chapter 12).

On the other hand, it is difficult to derive the bishops and deacons of 15:1 from extant Christian literature. In view of the Didachist's complete neglect of the Pauline letters, we would not expect him to pick up the reference from Philippians 1:1. Nor did he get it from the Book of Acts,[30] which habitually speaks of presbyters and only once

---

[30] Although Vokes, *op. cit.*, p. 150 f., refers to Acts 14:23.

refers to them as bishops (20:28); and certainly not from the Pastoral Epistles. The suggestion of 1 Clement 42:4 f. is somewhat better, in view of the liturgical contacts with that letter; and one may note the "apostles and bishops and teachers and deacons" of Hermas *Vis.* iii. 5. 1. 15:1 f. looks like a later addition to the sections on church officials, but how can it be *very* late if it does not also mention presbyters, who usually appear in second century writings? Would not both Catholic and Montanist churches have presbyters as well as bishops and deacons? The most probable supposition is that the author has some old source or tradition in which bishops and deacons are the leaders of the church, and which does not mention presbyters at all, at least not as a ministerial order. He tells nothing about them that is not said of the prophets and teachers; their qualifications must be the same. But they have a firm place in church life; hence a teaching of the Risen Christ to his apostles, which gives directions for church life, must at least mention them in passing.

The conclusion of the matter is that the Didache can very well be looked upon as an expansion of Matthew 28:19 f.: "Go then and make disciples of all the Gentiles, baptizing them into the name of the Father and of the Son and of the Holy Spirit, teaching them to observe whatever I have commanded you; and see, I am with you always, until the end of the age [*or* world]." It purports to be the Lord's teaching through the Twelve to the Gentiles. It tells how disciples are to be made (catechetical section, chapters 1–6), how they are to be baptized (chapter 7), and what the Lord has commanded them to observe (chapters 8–15), and finally it encourages them to wait for the end of the age (chapter 16).[31]

[31] Since writing the above, I have discovered that to some extent Zahn, *op. cit.*, p. 927, anticipates my conclusion.

ARCHAIC CRUCIFIXION ICONOGRAPHY

HAROLD RIDEOUT WILLOUGHBY

University of Chicago

Comparatively few are the iconologists on the American side of the Atlantic Ocean at the present time. There are many important and fascinating areas of investigation and research where American operations still have the freshness and thrill of pioneering work. This is particularly the case in matters so meticulous and subtle and detailed as stylism and iconography in art history.

Sound beginnings in iconographic research have been made in America, however, notably during the intra-World-War decades. To a considerable extent these have found the bulk of their resources analyzed and organized in the well-known Princeton Index of Christian Art.[1] This incomparable instrument for humanistic research had its inception in the period of World War I, and has had steadily increasing influence and usefulness ever since. A definite Princeton School of art historians has emerged and developed along with the Princeton Index itself. One main outcome of the activities of this group has been the creation of a corpus of *The Illustrations in Manuscripts of the Septuagint* under the joint editorship of Ernest T. DeWald, A. M. Friend, Jr., and Kurt Weitzmann.[2] Directly paralleling this is the Chicago corpus of *Text-Illustrations in Manuscripts of the Greek New Testament* that is being actively for-

[1] Helen Woodruff, *The Index of Christian Art at Princeton University* (Princeton, 1942).

[2] Ernest T. DeWald, *The Illustrations in the Manuscripts of the Septuagint, Part I: Vaticanus Graecus 1927* (Princeton, 1941); *Idem, Part II: Vaticanus Graecus 752* (Princeton, 1942). See also the Haskins Medal volume by Donald Drew Egbert, *The Tickhill Psalter and Related Manuscripts* (Princeton, 1940).

warded at the present time.[3] Professor Morey's well-articulated utilization of iconographic and stylistic data in reconstructing the main developments in *Early Christian Art* and in *Mediaeval Art* is most impressive and widely convincing.[4]

Actually an American project, though it materialized in Paris, was the Peirce-Tyler *répertoire* of dated and approximately datable Byzantine monuments.[5] It is most disadvantageous that world-wide depression choked off the publication of this series when only two folio volumes had appeared.

Of basic import for the veriest beginnings of Early Christian art and iconography have been the frescoes: pagan, Jewish, and Christian, uncovered by American archeologists at Dura-Europos on the Euphrates.[6] For years to come the specific importance of these frontier wall paintings will be matter for discussion.

In the area of mosaic painting the great American field project is the uncovering of the mosaics of Hagia Sophia in Instanbul by the Byzantine Institute, operating under the direction of Thomas Whittemore. Not even World

---

[3] Edgar J. Goodspeed, Donald W. Riddle, and Harold R. Willoughby, *The Rockefeller McCormick New Testament* (Chicago, 1932); Ernest Cadman Colwell and Harold R. Willoughby, *The Four Gospels of Karahissar* (Chicago, 1936); Harold R. Willoughby and Ernest Cadman Colwell, *The Elizabeth Day McCormick Apocalypse* (Chicago, 1940). See also Harold R. Willoughby, *The Rockefeller McCormick Manuscript and What Came of It: A Bibliographical Record* (Chicago, 1943).

[4] Charles R. Morey, *Early Christian Art* (Princeton, 1942); *Idem, Mediaeval Art* (New York, 1942).

[5] Hayford Peirce and Royall Tyler, *L'Art byzantin* (Paris, 1932–34).

[6] James Henry Breasted, *Oriental Forerunners of Byzantine Painting* (Chicago, 1924); C. Hopkins and P. V. C. Baur, *The Christian Church at Dura-Europos* (New Haven, 1934); H. F. Pearson, C. H. Kraeling, *et al., Preliminary Report on the Synagogue at Dura* (New Haven, 1936); M. Rostovtzeff, *Dura Europos and Its Art* (Oxford, 1938). See also Robert du Mesnil du Buisson, *Les Peintures de la synagogue de Doura-Europos* (Rome, 1939).

ARCHAIC CRUCIFIXION ICONOGRAPHY 125

War II put a period to Professor Whittemore's activities or his reports! [7]

For its implementation of iconographic studies in varied and far-extended fields, the Pierpont Morgan Library in New York City deserves great gratitude. Ever since this private library made its exceptional resources available to serious investigators, it has performed educational and research functions unique in America.[8]

In exactly the catastrophic period of World War II the superb resources of the Dumbarton Oaks Collection and Research Library have been most stimulating in actualizing the broad purposes for which the collection itself is currently being administered by Harvard University: "THAT THE CONTINUITY OF SCHOLARSHIP IN THE BYZANTINE AND MEDIAEVAL HUMANITIES MAY REMAIN UNBROKEN TO CLARIFY AN EVER CHANGING PRESENT AND TO INFORM THE FUTURE WITH WISDOM." In *Dumbarton Oaks Papers* to date, iconographic materials have been given full cognizance.[9]

It would be most ungracious, in this connection, not to cite recognition of the reënforcement to iconologic research in America that has come from foreign-trained scholars who have adopted the United States as their home.

[7] Thomas Whittemore, *The Mosaics of St. Sophia at Istanbul: The Mosaics of the Narthex* (Paris, 1933); Idem, *The Mosaics of St. Sophia at Istanbul: The Mosaics of the Southern Vestibule* (Paris, 1936); Idem, *The Mosaics of Hagia Sophia at Istanbul: The Imperial Portraits of the South Gallery* (Boston, 1942).

[8] See the reports of the Pierpont Morgan Library reviewing the activities of the library through half-decade periods since the middle twenties. For an example of recent research based on Morgan Library materials see Hanns Swarzenski, *The Berthold Missal* (New York, 1943). Frick Art Reference Library in New York City also deserves honorable mention for its organization of important materials for iconographic research.

[9] Henri Focillon, M. I. Rostovtzeff, C. R. Morey, and Wilhelm Koehler, *Dumbarton Oaks Inaugural Lectures* (Cambridge, 1941); Hayford Peirce and Royall Tyler, *Three Byzantine Works of Art* (Cambridge, 1941).

126   MUNERA STUDIOSA

Der Nersessian at Wellesley, Weitzmann and Panofsky at Princeton, and Paul Friedländer at the University of California in Los Angeles are outstanding savants who have added intense personal interest and exceptional technical equipment to the advancement of iconographic studies in our country and theirs.[10] For the future development of iconology in America, the establishment of the Pontifical Mediaeval Institute at St. Michael's in Toronto is a very promising circumstance.

Among American-born pioneers in this refined area of research, W. H. P. Hatch of the Episcopal Theological School in Cambridge, holds sure status. Special dependability may be accredited to his iconographic operations because they have always been solidly supported by technical competence in the science of paleography, in textual criticism, and in manuscript study generally. One of his early publications was his descriptions and collations, with C. C. Edmonds, of the tetraevangelia in the library of General Theological Seminary, New York City.[11] His descriptions included the painstaking notation of the miniatures and ornaments featured in these codices. Thereafter in his highly useful albums of New Testament MSS in Jerusalem or on Sinai, written in Greek uncials or minuscules, or in dated Syriac script, such descriptive notations were given proper prominence.[12] His publication of *Greek and Syrian*

---

[10] These should be regarded as typical titles only: Sirarpie Der Nersessian, *L'Illustration du roman de Barlaam et Joasaph* (Paris, 1937); Paul Friedländer, *Documents of Dying Paganism* (Berkeley, 1945); Erwin Panofsky, *Studies in Iconology* (New York, 1939); Kurt Weitzmann, *Die byzantinische Buchmalerei* (Berlin, 1935).

[11] C. C. Edmonds and W. H. P. Hatch, *The Gospel Manuscripts of the General Theological Seminary* (Cambridge, Mass., 1918).

[12] W. H. P. Hatch, *An Album of Dated Syriac Manuscripts* (Boston, 1946); *Idem, The Greek Manuscripts of the New Testament in Jerusalem* (Paris, 1934); *Idem, The Greek Manuscripts of the New Testament at Mount Sinai* (Paris, 1932); *Idem, The Principal Uncial Manuscripts of the New Testament* (Chicago, 1939).

ARCHAIC CRUCIFIXION ICONOGRAPHY

Miniatures in Jerusalem, produced under the auspices of the Mediaeval Academy of America in 1931, was characterized by full and accurate iconographic analyses. A concentrated Introduction to the descriptions surveyed the development of miniature painting in the Byzantine Empire. Currently we eagerly await the appearance of his volume on *The Miniatures of the Jerusalem Gregory Nazianzen* — another pathfinder into an unexplored area of iconologic study.

With emphasis on the exemplary character of his own manuscript studies, it is a privilege to salute Professor Hatch with the record of a single, detailed venture in iconographic research, involving a very problematic and a very important little codex of the Gospel of Mark.

The manuscript in question has nowhere been published, though it has been listed in a catalogue and very infrequently noticed otherwise.[13] Its problematic idiosyncrasies have never been completely canvassed. The full stature of its importance: paleographic, iconographic, and textual, has never been comprehensively estimated.

This most peculiar of Marcan codices is now in the Rare Book Room of the University of Chicago, where it is numbered MS 972 in the University's collection. In the central Gregory-Eltester catalogue of New Testament MSS it is accessioned as Codex 2427. Because of the dramatic archaisms that distinguish alike its contents and its pictures and even its phenomenal script, it is known locally as the Archaic Gospel of Mark.

[13] K. W. Clark, *A Descriptive Catalogue of Greek New Testament Manuscripts in America* (Chicago, 1937), p. 271; Ernest Cadman Colwell, "An Ancient Text of the Gospel of Mark," *Emory University Quarterly*, Vol. 1, No. 2 (June, 1945), pp. 65–75; Harold R. Willoughby, *The Four Gospels of Karahissar* (Chicago, 1936), Vol. II, *passim; Idem, The Rockefeller McCormick New Testament* (Chicago, 1932), III, 124–125, Pl. XLII. At the present time Ernest Cadman Colwell, Allen P. Wikgren, and Harold R. Willoughby are collaborating on the comprehensive publication of this baffling but obviously significant manuscript.

Chicago MS 972 was first brought to American attention a decade and a half ago by Mlle. Sirarpie Der Nersessian of Collège de France and Wellesley College, who referred us for information concerning it to M. André Xyngopoulos, at that time Ephor of the Greek government for Byzantine antiquities. The Ephor sent us a breath-taking series of line drawings reproducing faithfully the seventeen miniatures in the codex.[14] These reproductions were themselves masterpieces, rendered in the classical manner of John Flaxman and Mme. Sophie Millet. Concerning the location of the MS the Ephor reported: "se trouvait il y a 5 ans dans une collection privée à Athènes. Maintenant son possesseur est parti d'Athènes et je ne sais plus maintenant où se trouve le MS."[15] Accordingly the earliest printed references to these fascinating miniatures designated them individually as *Privatbesitz*.

In 1937 the codex itself appeared in America, and was offered for purchase to the University of Chicago. Through the joint efforts of Edgar J. Goodspeed and Ernest Cadman Colwell it was acquired by the University.

The text of Codex 2427 is only the Gospel of Mark in Greek — nothing more: no manuscript equipment, no marginalia, no colophons. In fact the only writing in this codex in addition to the gospel text itself is simply the book title in antique form and in gilded letters:

ΕΤΑΓΓΕΛΙΟΝ ΚΑΤΑ ΜΑΡΚΟΝ

The first page and the last folio of the codex are complete blanks.

[14] Plate II is a facsimile of one of these line drawings.

[15] Here is the statement of M. Xyngopoulos concerning the pre-Athens history of Codex 2427: "Sur la provenance de ce manuscrit je ne sais que peu de choses. Il appartenait autrefois à un antiquaire, entre les mains duquel je l'ai vu. Cet antiquaire, déjà mort, étant originaire de Cappadoce et ayant beaucoup de relations avec l'Asie Mineure, on pourrait supposer que ce manuscrit proviendrait d'Anatolie." Letter dated "Athènes le 18 Décembre 1939."

PLATE I

CODEX 2427   CHICAGO MS 972

THE CRUCIFIXION

PLATE II

CODEX 2427　　　　　　　　　　CHICAGO MS 972

THE CRUCIFIXION
(After Xyngopoulos)

ARCHAIC CRUCIFIXION ICONOGRAPHY 129

The Gospel is contained in a remarkably small, hand-sized volume measuring in cover size 3⅜ x 5⅛ inches, and in page size averaging about 3⅜ x 4⅝ inches. These miniature proportions are not quite so exceptional in Greek manuscripts as it seems at first. Such minute codices are known from the earliest book era and they seem to have been relatively more numerous in the latest Greek manuscript period.

The folios number 44, making 88 pages altogether. One union of folios, nos. 17 and 24, is exceptionally ruled at right angles to the lines of writing of the present text. This was done for a larger manuscript than ours. The parchment of Chicago MS 972 is rather coarse and noticeably uneven in thickness. It is closely mottled with brown blotches that bespeak fungal deterioration.

In structure Codex 2427 consists of five regular quaternions followed by one binion at the very end of the book. A quaternion of eight leaves is the standard gathering most familiar to students of medieval Greek manuscripts. From the point of view of its quire system, this little codex is quite regularly organized. The few quaternions of Chicago MS 972 are among the very few normal features of the book.

The folios are very loosely bound together within blind-stamped covers of dark brown goatskin. The patterns of the stamped areas persist in varying degrees of obliteration. Enough remain to indicate the prime circumstance that the stamps themselves were Greek-monastic in origin. Some of them were identical with stamps used on the covers of the McCormick Apocalypse at the University of Chicago,[16] and on the Gennadius *Epitaphion* by Gregory of Nyssa at

---

[16] Harold R. Willoughby, "Greek Rebinding Colophons in Chicago Manuscripts," *Annales de l'Institut Kondakov* (Seminarium Kondakovianum), XI (1939), 21–32, Pl. IX; *Idem, McCormick Apocalypse*, I, 48–82, Pls. I–III.

the American School of Classical Studies in Athens.[17] A reconstruction of overall pattern on the covers of Codex 2427 shows that they were originally intended for use on a much larger book. None too skillfully they were cut down in adaptation to the Archaic Gospel of Mark.

The text of MS 972 was written in a single column per page; double-spaced on the first folio, and single-spaced thereafter. Such initial double-spacing in a manuscript book was essentially a decorative expedient, known in manuscripts in other languages than Greek, and best known, perhaps, in ornate Armenian codices.

The number of text lines per page varies signally in Chicago MS 972. On single-spaced pages it runs as high as 26 and as low as 20, with 21-line pages most numerous and 22-line pages next most numerous. These line variations are flouted in the face of the reader. They appear on opposite sides of single folios, and on facing pages between two folios.

The script in which Codex 2427 is penned is the despair of the trained paleographer. This is not at all the usual Byzantine book hand. It is crude, irregular, choppy, uneven, difficult to read. In the experience of those who have worked closely with it, this script is *sui generis* in its most distinctive features. As Greek writing it is extremely provincial, even verging into barbarity.

President Colwell[18] emphasizes the following as unique, or nearly unique usages of this scribe: abbreviating the definite article in one way or another, doubling certain consonants by making superior strokes, and accomplishing unusual ligatures between letters. Modern writing practices, almost unknown in medieval Greek script, are his use of periods to designate abbreviations and his habit of dividing his text into words.

[17] Lucy Allen Paton, *Selected Bindings from the Gennadius Library* (Cambridge, Mass., 1924), pp. 2-3, Pl. IV.
[18] *Emory University Quarterly*, Vol. I, No. 2 (June, 1945), pp. 68-69.

Distinctly late antique rather than medieval are the abbreviations of the *nomina sacra* in this Gospel manuscript. This appears especially in the choice of words given *nomina-sacra* abbreviation by the omission of their middle letters. Only a very small group of potent terms are thus regularly abbreviated: God, Lord, Christ, and Jesus. On the other hand, some few very exceptional words are thus occasionally abbreviated: John, King, Holy, and Disciple. This scribe has left a conspicuously idiosyncratic record, some of it reminiscent of late antique or early Christian usages in Gospel copying.

The overmastering significance of Chicago MS 972 that has emerged to date is the quality and type of the Greek text of the Gospel that it preserves. Here is an obviously late manuscript of the Marcan Gospel; but the type of its Greek text had currency at least one thousand years earlier than this codex was written. By detailed statistical comparison it can be demonstrated that the text of Archaic Mark is closer to the great Codex Vaticanus, than is Codex Sinaiticus itself. This was the distinctive character of our Marcan text that first impressed the discerning mind of Professor Goodspeed, and it has become more and more emphatic with detailed investigation. Neutral or Alexandrian Text, Old Uncial or Beta Text are the impressive classification labels that might approximately be applied to this rendering of the Gospel of Mark. Nevertheless the most obvious feature of Codex Vaticanus in the Second Gospel, ending abruptly at 16:8, is not a feature of the Chicago Codex. It includes the so-called "long conclusion" to the Gospel.

"The most sensational readings of the Chicago Mark" — to quote the evaluation of President Colwell [19] — are unique omissions from the familiar text of the shortest of the gospels. Many of these brief readings leave out parenthetical

[19] *Ibid.*, pp. 72–75.

and explanatory matter that seems to be secondary in relation to the main subject matter. Examples are the omission of the explanation about the ablutions of the Pharisees at Mark 7:3-4, and the omission of the parenthesis "the reader must take note of this" from Mark 13:14. It must be said that the great majority of these short readings strike the mind as being intrinsically primitive in character.

From sheer lack of determinative evidence it is impossible to be definite about the date of this fascinating manuscript. The general impression is that it must be considerably late in the Byzantine period. Some specific iconographic data and features of antique revivalism emerging in the miniatures seem to point to the fourteenth century in the Paleologan period as the time of writing. M. Xyngopoulos so recorded his estimate of the date on the basis of the style of writing — "d'après l'écriture." From the study of a photograph Kirsopp Lake inclined to date it even later; but from an inspection of the manuscript itself he concluded "it might be as early as the thirteenth century."

Fully as obscure as the date is the question of provenance. This crude codex was certainly not a Constantinopolitan or centrally Byzantine production. Its phenomenal peculiarities mark it as provincial and even ultra-provincial in origin. Plenty of evidence can be adduced to classify it as an eastern provincial product, rather than western. As to specific locale, however, it is difficult to be explicit. Data can be cited: technical, stylistic, and iconographic, that point to the Trapezuntine area as the *Gebiet* of this codex. M. Xyngopoulos is of the opinion that it was from Asia Minor that the Codex was brought to Athens in the recent period.[20]

As problematic and as challenging as script or text are the tempera miniatures that enliven Codex 2427. Perhaps they have relatively equal importance with the Archaic Marcan text even. These paintings are seventeen in num-

[20] See note 15.

ber, including one Evangelist portrait and sixteen text illustrations. The latter are tiny tableaux, square to oblong in format, with gold backgrounds and linear orange-red frames. Regularly they are ensconced within the panel of the single column of text that they illustrate. The locations and themes of these paintings are as follows:

Folio	Subject	Text
1 verso,	The Evangelist Mark,	Mark 1:1–3
4 verso,	The Cure of Simon's Mother-in-law,	Mark 1:29–31
5 verso,	The Capernaum Paralytic Forgiven,	Mark 2:1–5
12 recto,	Jairus' Daughter Restored to Life,	Mark 5:40, 41
15 verso,	The Multiplication of the Loaves and Fishes,	Mark 6:38–42
19 verso,	The Cure of the Bethsaida Blind Man,	Mark 8:22–25
21 recto,	The Transfiguration,	Mark 9:3, 4, 7
27 recto,	The Triumphal Entry,	Mark 11:7–10
34 verso,	The Last Supper,	Mark 14:17–21
37 verso,	Jesus before Pilate,	Mark 15:1–5
38 recto,	Barabbas or Jesus?	Mark 15:6–15a
38 verso,	Roman Soldiers Mock Jesus,	Mark 15:16–19
39 recto,	Simon of Cyrene carries Jesus' Cross,	Mark 15:20, 21
39 verso,	The Crucifixion of Jesus with Two Thieves,	Mark 15:25–41
40 recto,	Four Young Men Dice for Jesus' Clothes,	Mark 15:24
41 verso,	Joseph of Arimathea Asks for the Corpse of Jesus,	Mark 15:42–45
42 recto,	The Marcan Young Man at the Empty Tomb,	Mark 16:1–7

Of these seventeen Gospel miniatures, two only are full-page paintings: the Evangelist portrait and the Crucifixion tableau. The former has a classical and pagan quality that completely sets it apart from the series of scenes that it introduces. The latter, in its distinguishing characteristics, is really typical of the Marcan illustration cycle of which it is a part. Accordingly we proceed to analyze the iconography of this full-page Crucifixion tableau (Plate I), noting with emphasis the typical features that it exemplifies. Incidentally, these are the very aspects of the painting that especially are creative of problems, both art-historical and religious-historical.

Indubitably this rendering of the Crucifixion is the most distinguished text-illustration in Chicago MS 972. The student who has lived a long time with this painting, and devoted careful attention to its characteristic features, cannot escape the conclusion that here in small scale is a very great depiction of a most important theme. Both compositionally and iconographically it will bear comparison with the highly significant and early paintings of the spectacle on the cover of the Sancta Sanctorum reliquary in the Vatican,[21] and in the famed Rabula Gospels of the Laurenziana.[22] Because of its quality and import, it is to be reproduced in full color in the definitive edition of Codex 2427. From the point of view of the composition as a whole it recalls very ancient pictorial representations of the tragedy. At the same time it records detailed features of iconography that seem quite peculiar and are certainly difficult to explain.[23]

[21] Hartmann Grisar, *Die römische Kapelle Sancta Sanctorum und ihr Schatz* (Freiburg, i.B., 1908), p. 115, Bild 59; Wilhelm Worringer, Heribert Reiners, und Leopold Seligmann (Eds.), *Festschrift zum sechzigsten Geburtstag von Paul Clemen* (Bonn, 1926), p. 162, Fig. 13.

[22] Guido Biagi, *Reproductions de manuscrits enluminés . . . de la Bibliothèque Medicea Laurenziana* (Florence, 1914), p. 7, Pl. I; Worringer, Reiners, und Seligmann, *Festschrift Clemen*, p. 150, Fig. 1.

[23] The following is a drastically selective bibliography on Crucifixion iconography: L. Bréhier, *Les Origines du Crucifix* (Paris, 1908); Vénétia Cottas, *L'Influence du drame "Christos paschon" sur l'art Chrétien d'Orient* (Paris, 1931), pp. 42–46, 72–79; Ernst Diez and Otto Demus, *Byzantine Mosaics in Greece: Hosios Lucas and Daphni* (Cambridge, Mass., 1931), pp. 67–69; Michael Engles, *Die Kreuzigung Christi in der bildenden Kunst* (Luxemburg, 1899); R. Forrer und G. A. Müller, *Kreuz und Kreuzigung Christi in ihrer Kunstentwicklung* (Strassburg, 1894); G. de Jerphanion,

ARCHAIC CRUCIFIXION ICONOGRAPHY

The total crucifixion composition in Archaic Mark may conveniently be analyzed in terms of the pairs of figures that supplement and support the central crucified form of Christ himself (see Plates I and II). Basically this is the execution of Jesus of Nazareth between two thieves. The two stark, black crosses of the thieves coordinate with the heavier central cross of Jesus himself to constitute an architectural framework for the tableau. Supplementing the widespread black crosses above are two pairs of vertical figures below. On either side of the focal cross of Jesus are operative the two lively youthful soldiers, red-headed and in red uniforms: Longinus with his λόγχη and Esopos with his ὕσσωπος. Together at the left stand the contrasting passive figures of the two intimate witnesses: the Theotokos all in black and the Beloved Disciple all in white. The dramatic effectiveness of this total pairing of figures is inescapable. From the outset it is worth remembering that in the long history of representations of the Crucifixion, these various pairs of personages were more frequently paired in separate pictures than in one and the same composition as here.

La Voix des monuments (Paris, 1930), pp. 138–164; *Idem, La Voix des monuments, nouvelle série* (Paris, 1938), pp. 255–262; C. Kennedy, *The Crucifix: An Outline Sketch of its History* (London, 1917); Karl Künstle, *Iconographie der Christlichen Kunst* (Freiburg i. B., 1926–28), I, 446–476; Béla Lázár, *Die beiden Wurzeln der Kruzifixdarstellungen* (Strassburg, 1912); Raimond van Marle, *Recherches sur l'iconographie de Giotto et de Duccio* (Strasbourg, 1920), pp. 35–37; Gabriel Millet, *Recherches sur l'iconographie de l'Évangile* (Paris, 1916), pp. 396–460; C. R. Morey, "The Painted Panel from the Sancta Sanctorum," *Festschrift Clemen* (Bonn, 1926), pp. 150–167; N. P. Pokrovsky, *The Gospels in Monuments of Iconography* (In Russian, St. Petersburg, 1892), pp. 314–385; Johannes Reil, *Christus am Kreuz in der Bildkunst der Karolingerzeit* (Leipzig, 1930); *Idem, Die frühchristlichen Darstellungen der Kreuzigung Christi* (Leipzig, 1904); Dorothy C. Shorr, "The Mourning Virgin and St. John," *Art Bulletin*, XXII (1940), 61–69; E. Soyez, *La Croix et le crucifix* (Amiens, 1910); Josef Wilpert, *Die römischen Mosaïken und Malereien der kirchlichen Bauten* (Freiburg i.B., 1924), II, 874–85.

It is rather disconcerting to observe that outstanding features of this Marcan miniature were Johannine rather than Synoptic in their ultimate derivation. The Beloved Disciple and the Theotokos were the distinctive Johannine witnesses to the tragedy. Synoptic Evangelists indicated loyal Galilean women observing the execution from a distance. The soldier who stabbed Jesus' side with his λόγχη was solely and typically a Johannine character in that action (Jn. 19:34). Also it was the ὕσσωπος of John 19:29 that gave to the warmhearted sponge-bearer his traditional Greek name "Esopos." [24] For an illustration to a Marcan text, this full-page painting includes a surprising number of peculiar and literal Johannine details.

Matching the prominence of Fourth Gospel characters in this tableau is the conspicuous absence of typical Synoptic personages from it. This Marcan scene does not exhibit the jeering passers-by, or the mocking scribes and priests, or the testifying centurion, or the faithful Galilean women, all of whom are specified in the terse Marcan narrative itself (Mk. 15:29–41). Both by its omissions and by its inclusions the Crucifixion scene in Codex 2427 is demonstrably more Johannine than it is Marcan or Synoptic.

More important is it to recall that the Johannine pairing of characters in the 2427 Crucifixion corresponds exactly to the earliest known representational schemes for the tableau extant in early Christian monuments today. In period these early pictorial representations of the Crucifixion emerge as early as the fifth and sixth centuries. They exist numerously today, and in a variety of media: metal work, sculpture, painting, and specifically manuscript illustrations. This most ancient pictorial type for the Crucifixion is classed by art historians as "antique Syrian," from its early period and its near-Eastern provenance.

M. Gabriel Millet, in his encyclopedic *Recherches sur*

---

[24] In the Catholic West the Latins called him Stephaton.

ARCHAIC CRUCIFIXION ICONOGRAPHY 137

l'iconographie de l'évangile presents the following concentrated analysis of this archaic organization of the Crucifixion tableau: "L'ancienne iconographie syrienne a créé une composition complexe, symétrique et symbolique, d'après le quatrième évangile, à l'exclusion des synoptiques. Elle représenta d'abord Jésus crucifié entre deux larrons (Jn. 19:18-22). . . . Marie et Jean (25-27), ou bien, le porte-éponge (28-30) et le coup de lance (31-37), enfin, ces deux groupes ensemble." [25]

The chief exemplars of the "antique Syrian" organization of the Crucifixion are so notably reputable as to demand specific citation. For the total ensemble, including all three pairs of subsidiary figures, we have the two great paintings already cited together: the Crucifixion page in the Rabula Gospels of 586 and the painted frieze on the reliquary cover in the Sancta Sanctorum treasure. Also an encolpion at Monza comprehends all three pairs of Johannine characters.[26] For the structural framework of three crucified figures, Jesus between two thieves, there can be cited numerous metal censers, the panel of carved wood in the Santa Sabina doors on the Aventine, and Choricius' often-cited description of the St. Sergius mosaic in Gaza.[27] For the Johannine pair of the intimate witnesses, the Beloved Disciple and the Sorrowing Mother, there are various censers and the Monza ampullae.[28] Finally, the merciful actions of the two soldiers, Esopos and Longinus, were depicted on a Bobbio ampulla and on the splendid metal plate found at Perm.[29] Monuments with which the student of Early Christian iconography has repeatedly to deal ex-

[25] Millet, *Recherches*, p. 423.
[26] R. Garrucci, *Storia dell'arte Cristiana* (Prato, 1872-81), Vol. VI, Pl. 433, No. 4.
[27] "They have finally consigned him to the vilest of all deaths, between a pair of thieves."
[28] Garrucci, *Storia*, Vol. VI, Pl. 434, Nos. 2 and 6.
[29] Reil, *Kreuzigung*, Pl. II.

emplify the "antique Syrian" type of Crucifixion painted in Chicago MS 972.

The precise pairing of Fourth-Gospel actors, distinctive of the ancient Syrian picturization of the Crucifixion, contrasted extremely with the medieval developments of the theme in Byzantine circles. Curiously two mutually reversed and entirely antithetical Byzantine developments in the later centuries are distinguishable. One trend complicated the spectacle endlessly by the intrusion of Synoptic personages. The other trend simplified the tableau to the nth degree by excluding all but the very most important and typical Johannine personages.

Chronologically earlier was the Byzantine amplification of the Crucifixion spectacle. By the introduction of individuals and groups derived from Synoptic narratives the scene was made more lively and picturesque and spectacular and dramatic. A small group of Galilean women was introduced, balancing the Theotokos. The declamatory Roman centurion matched the passive Beloved Disciple. Scoffing priests and soldiers and scribes and nondescripts crowded in from one or another of the Synoptic Gospels. The great poly-friezed Byzantine Tetraevangelia gave influential currency to this Synoptic enlargement of the Crucifixion spectacle,[30] and Athonite frescoes perpetuated the pageant in the post-Byzantine era.[31]

Equally Byzantine was the reduction of the tableau to the symmetrical simplicity and integrity of a three-figure composition. Two by two the pairs of Fourth-Gospel personages on whom the ancient Syrian rendering placed emphasis

[30] Henri Omont, *Évangiles avec peintures byzantines du XI siècle* (Paris, n.d.). Pls. 50–52, 87–88, 140, 178–180.
[31] Gabriel Millet, *Monuments de l'Athos* (Paris, 1927), Pl. 12, No. 3 (Protaton); Pl. 69, No. 2 (Chilandari; Pl. 79, No. 1 (Chilandari); Pl. 83, No. 2 (Vatopedi); Pl. 129, Nos. 1 and 2 (Lavra); Pl. 162, No. 1 (Kutlumusi); Pl. 174, No. 3 (Xenophon); Pl. 181, No. 1 (Xenophon); Pl. 189, No. 3 (St. Paul); Pl. 264, No. 1 (Skite of Xenophon).

ARCHAIC CRUCIFIXION ICONOGRAPHY 139

were eliminated from the scene altogether. Even the crucified thieves were removed, leaving the cross of Jesus standing in solitary grimness. Both the soldier with the lance and the soldier with the hyssop were ostracized. There remained only the crucified Christ, with the Theotokos standing at his right and Beloved Disciple standing at his left. The most surely unforgettable Byzantine rendering of the three-figure Crucifixion was the unequalled Daphni mosaic.[32] Judging from the numbers of extant monuments in practically all media of artistic expression, the three-figure Crucifixion was the most-favored Byzantine manner of picturing the execution of Jesus. In entirely different ways the Byzantine enlargements and reduction of the Crucifixion scene accent for us the antiquity of the Syrian scheme for the tableau exemplified in Chicago MS 972.

As a total composition, then, the 2427 Crucifixion is demonstrably antique Syrian in ultimate origin. There are, however, particular and obvious details in this rendering of the ancient scheme that are very peculiar and very puzzling. One is the pairing of the Theotokos and the Beloved Disciple together at the left (from the spectator's viewpoint), instead of distributing them symmetrically, one on the left and the other on the right.[33] This gives a strong un-Byzantine stress of asymmetry to the scene.

In explanation of the phenomenon it must be remembered, first of all, that the Fourth Gospel text itself placed together in most intimate fashion the Mother and the Disciple.[34] Any literal illustration of that text would picture together, rather than separately, these two faithful personages.

In the second place, there are plenty of great examples,

[32] Diez and Demus, *Hosios Lucas and Daphni*, Fig. 99; Gabriel Millet, *Le monastère de Daphni* (Paris, 1899), Pl. XVI.
[33] See Pls. I and II.
[34] Jn. 19:26, 27.

early and later, in various major groups of monuments, that illustrate this intimate juxtaposition. The prime early Syrian example is precisely the Rabula Crucifixion of 586.[35] Among the South Gaul-North Italian ivories, investigated so expertly by Baldwin Smith, the British Museum passion panel of the fifth century thus brackets the Disciple and the Mother.[36] Cappadocian examples could be cited from Toqale and Tchouch In, and from psalters of the Chludov class. Central Constantinopolitan renderings are preserved in the fully illustrated tetraevangelia, Laur. VI. 23 and Paris 74, and in the choicely illustrated Athens 93 — incidentally the closest iconographic cognate to Chicago MS 972 that has been isolated to date. Thus a surprising amount of ancient and reputable exemplification can be found for the intimate juxtaposition of the Theotokos and the Disciple in the Crucifixion scene of Chicago MS 972.

Distinct in the Chicago Crucifixion miniature is the facial contrast between the "good thief" Dysmas (or Demas), and the "bad thief" Gestas.[37] The former, on Christ's right, is smooth faced and good looking. The latter, on Christ's left, is hirsute in black and bristly fashion. Most inhumanly his face has been piously obliterated. It is a sure inference that originally he was villainous looking. This pictorial antithesis had sound textual basis. The third canonical gospel, with its peculiar passion source, started the character-destroying process by contrasting the abusive criminal with the praying criminal.[38] Apocryphal gospels completed the process by naming the criminals and narrating concrete good and bad deeds that they had done.[39] In the long

[35] Biagi, *loc. cit.*
[36] O. M. Dalton, *Catalogue of Ivory Carvings of the Christian Era . . . in the British Museum* (London, 1909), No. 7, pp. 5 f., Pl. IV.
[37] See again Plates I and II.
[38] Lk. 23:39–43.
[39] Among the apocryphal books read particularly the *Gospel of Nicodemus* or *Acts of Pilate*, and also the *Story of Joseph of Arimathaea*.

ARCHAIC CRUCIFIXION ICONOGRAPHY 141

history of East Christian manuscript illustration, the pictorial contrast between the "good thief" and the "bad thief," began at least as early as the dated Rabula Gospels. This detailed contrast in the Chicago Crucifixion miniatures is, again, an "antique Syrian" feature.

The sharp angularity and crass distortion of Christ's body on the cross are inescapable and unforgettable features of the Chicago Crucifixion scene.[40] Such was not the early Syrian treatment of Jesus' crucified body. The arms horizontal and the body vertical, at right angles to each other, summarized the antique Syrian way of disposing Jesus' body on the cross. Nor was this agonized angularity typical of the suave Byzantine statement of the posture during the Middle Ages. The arms in a down-curving segment of a circle, and the body swerving in a reverse letter S, constituted the refined Byzantine arrangement.

Angular distortions such as this were, however, characteristic of Oriental versions from the Greek: Slavonic, Georgian, Armenian, and Syrian. The very closest counterpart we can name to the crucified Christ in MS 972 is an Armenian Christ in MS 1193 at San Lazarro, Venice.[41] Plenty of approximations might be specified from other Near Eastern manuscripts. M. Millet thus described the distribution of the type: "Il appartient à l'Orient, car il y a suivi le chemin accoutumé.... Syrie, Arménie, Géorgie, Russie." [42] Oriental influence seems to account for the angularity of Christ's body in the 2427 Crucifixion tableau.

More problematic are the lowering gray clouds edged with white that sweep across the sky in the Chicago miniature.[43] True Byzantine Crucifixions never included clouds — far from it! One recalls the twin hills that give depth

[40] Compare Pls. I and II.
[41] Sirarpie Der Nersessian, *Manuscrits arméniens illustres .... de Venise* (Paris, 1937), Pl. XXVIII.
[42] Millet, *Recherches*, p. 414.
[43] Examine Pls. I and II.

and perspective to the Crucifixion tableaux in the Rabula Gospels and on the Sancta Sanctorum reliquary. But clouds are not hills and vice versa. Again it is in Oriental-language manuscripts of the late medieval period that we find clouds adding murky grimness to the Crucifixion scene. These seem to be relatively more numerous in Armenian manuscripts than in other Oriental versions. There the examples both antedate and follow the period of Codex 2427. The most decoratively conventionalized clouds known to us in any painting of the Crucifixion hang suspended in a Mongoloid miniature belonging to the Kurdian Collection in Wichita, Kansas.[44] From the noticeable frequency of clouds above Crucifixions in the Oriental versions, we infer that late medieval influences from the Christian East may account for this feature in our miniature.

Most problematic of all is the sun in process of eclipse — a white lunette gleaming on the edge of a black disc — above the Chicago Crucifixion.[45] It illustrates, of course, the Synoptic tradition that, "At noon darkness spread over the whole country, and lasted until three in the afternoon." [46] The eclipse is here pictured quite simply and distinctly in progress. For all its simplicity, however, no duplicate of this picturization of the phenomenon has yet been isolated, early or late, in the east or west. How is this apparently unique depiction to be explained?

By far the most explicit and picturesque account of the Crucifixion eclipse composed in Greek was the narrative of Pseudo-Dionysius the Areopagite which described "how we saw the obscuration itself start from the east, advance to the circumference of the sun, and at length withdraw. Furthermore we saw the darkening and the clearing take

---

[44] H. Kurdian, "An Armenian MS with Unique Mongolian Miniatures," *Journal of the Royal Asiatic Society* XVII (April, 1941), 145-148, Pl. II.
[45] *Noch einmal* Pls. I and II.
[46] Mt. 27:45; Mk. 15:33; Lk. 23:44.

ARCHAIC CRUCIFIXION ICONOGRAPHY 143

place not in the same direction, but in exactly the opposite direction." [47]

This description by Pseudo-Dionysius is known to have been iconographically influential in the Middle Ages in both the Christian West and the Christian East. From the West there is the attestation of a superb series of works of art by the School of St. Denis, identified by A. M. Friend, Jr.[48] From the East there is the picture in the famous Chludov Psalter showing Dionysius himself indicating with astonishment the phenomenal character of the eclipse.[49]

Realistically it seems to be a moment in the process of eclipse as described in detail by Pseudo-Dionysius, either the obscuring or the clearing, that is pictured in the Chicago Crucifixion miniature. Accordingly we suggest that this simple, but singular feature of the scene may be another outstanding example of the extraordinary influence of Pseudo-Dionysius the Areopagite in the field of medieval iconography.

Altogether a very fascinating combination of elements, structural and incidental, are presented to the student of iconology by the Crucifixion painting in Codex 2427. The general organization of the spectacle is Early Christian and specifically antique Syrian. Some of the individual motifs, like the bristly beard of the "bad thief" Gestas, are also demonstrably early Christian in initial expression. Other detailed renderings, like the angularity of Christ's body, are medieval Oriental statements. One peculiar phenom-

---

[47] The passage quoted in translation is from *Letter VII, To Polycarp of Smyrna.* For the Greek text see J. P. Migne, *Patrologiae cursus completus, series Graeca,* Tome 3 (Paris, 1857), Col. 1081.

[48] A. M. Friend, Jr., "Carolingian Art in the School of St. Denis," *Art Studies: Medieval, Renaissance, and Modern* I (1923), 67-75.

[49] The citation in the Chludov Psalter is: Moscow, Historical Museum, Gr. 129, fol. 45v. See also Nicolas Malickij, "Remarques sur la date des mosaïques de l'église des Saints-Apôtres à Constantinople décrits par Mésaritès," *Byzantion* III (1926), Fasc. 1, Pl. II, pp. 142-47.

enon, the sun in process of eclipse, may be influenced by a special source, the Pseudo-Dionysius description of the Crucifixion eclipse. Such diverse combinations of elements: early Christian, medieval Oriental, and peculiar realistic are to be found generally among the other pictures in the illustration cycle of Chicago MS 972.

Detailed iconographic analyses of all the miniatures in the Chicago codex have been completed and await publication with the facsimile reproductions of the paintings themselves. These analyses disclose that predominantly the illustrations of Archaic Mark are characterized by antiquity of composition and iconography, and by representational literalism in relation to Gospel texts. The literalisms in this Marcan series, however, are as frequently Johannine as they are Synoptic. In this matter the Crucifixion scene is eminently representative of the series of which it is a part. Compared with elements antique and literal, the medieval intrusions in these miniatures are less important and numerous, and usually they are quite distinguishable. In view of these conglomerate characteristics, it is certain that the series of pictures in Codex 2427 has much to tell us concerning the medieval transmission of Gospel illustration cycles in Greek manuscripts. In view of the preponderant increment of antique elements involved, it is probable that the miniatures have even more to tell us about the ultimate origins of Gospel illustration cycles in the Early Christian period.

NOTES ON BOOK-BURNING

ARTHUR STANLEY PEASE
Harvard University

The burning of books, practiced among the Hebrews as early as the time of Jeremiah, in Greco-Roman tradition from the fifth century B.C., and continuing to the age of the Spanish Inquisition and that of Nazi conflagrations in Berlin in 1933, has been discussed by various writers,[1] and it is not my purpose to retraverse all the ground they have covered, but rather, by typical earlier illustrations, to suggest one or two overlooked causes for the custom.

These burnings are occasionally due to an author himself, who orders a letter or other document to be burned after reading, for purposes of security,[2] or to express his dissatisfaction with an inferior [3] or unrecognized [4] performance or with the incomplete condition of a work at the time of his death.[5] But the most frequent agents of destruction have

---

[1] *E.g.*, for antiquity: T. Birt. *Das ant. Buchwesen* (Berlin, 1882), p. 369; C. A. Forbes in *Trans. Am. philol. Assoc.* LXVII (1936), 114–125; F. A. Sochatoff in *Class. Outlook* XVI (1939), 82. For later periods: F. G. Peignot, *Dict. crit., litt., et bibliogr. des principaux livres condamnés au feu*, etc., 2 vols. (Paris, 1806); I. D'Israeli, *Curiosities of Lit.*² (London, 1867), pp. 17–21; H. C. Lea, *Hist. of the Inquisition*, 3 vols. (New York, 1888), index, s.vv. *Books, Burning*; J. A. Farrer, *Books condemned to be burned* (London, 1892); H. C. Lea, *The Inquisition in the Spanish Dependencies* (New York, 1908), p. 70. Two or three helpful references and suggestions I owe to my colleague, Dr. Herbert Bloch.

[2] *E.g.*, Plat. *Ep.* 2, 314c (to Dionysius). Cf. Sen. Rhet. *Suas.* 6. 14: *deliberat Cicero an salutem promittente Antonio orationes suas comburat*; also *Suas.* 7, especially sections 4, 10, and 11.

[3] Apul. *Apol.* 10; Diog. L. III 5; Eustath. in *Il.* 18, 392 – these cases referring to the poems of the youthful Plato; possibly the case described by Suid. s.v. Μαρῖνος should be here classified.

[4] Juv. 7.22–25.

[5] So the sister of Empedocles, presumably in accordance with his own wish, burned his unfinished poem on the Persian Wars (Diog. L. VIII 57), and the dying Virgil commanded the burning of the unfinished *Aeneid*

been, not dissatisfied authors, but rulers, philosophers, or theologians, who have detected in the offending volumes the perils of seditious or heretical ideas.

Though my interest in the present article is primarily with religious and philosophical cases, it may be remarked that instances with a political basis seem to begin with the burning of Jeremiah's prophetic roll in the presence of King Jehoiakim,[5a] though more obviously political are the burning, in the early Empire, by decree of the senate, of the historical and other works of certain writers of outspoken republican sympathies, such as Titus Labienus, Cremutius Cordus, and Cassius Severus.[6] Later, under Domitian, falls the public burning of encomia upon the philosophers Paetus Thrasea and Helvidius Priscus by Arulenus Rusticus and

---

(Plin. *N.H.* VII 114; Favorinus ap. Gell. XVII 10.7; Donat. *Vit. Verg.* p. 9. Brummer; *Vita Gudiana* I, p. 61 Brummer; Servius, *Vita*, p. 70 Brummer; Servius Varus in Prob. *Vita*, p. 74 Brummer; *Anth. Lat.* I, no. 242 Riese; Sulp. Carthag. in *Anth. Lat.* II, no. 653, praef., Riese; [Augustus] in *Anth. Lat.* II, no. 672 Riese), an action theatrically imitated by Ovid with his *Metamorphoses* before he started into exile (*Tr.* I 7.15–26; IV 10.61–64; cf. Forbes, *op. cit.* pp. 115–116; also Quintil. *Inst.* VI proem. 3. So also perhaps Petrarch with the MS. of his *Africa*; cf. E. H. R. Tatham, *Francesco Petrarca*, (London, 1926), II, 174; at any rate Niccolò de' Niccoli said that Petrarch would have done better to burn it (cf. R. P. Oliver in *Class. Stud. in Honor of W. A. Oldfather* [Urbana, 1943], p. 146). Picturesque is the expression of Galen, VII 507 Kühn, inviting authors to invoke Hephaestus against the books which they repented of having written.

[5a] Jer. 36.1–32; Joseph. *Ant.* X 95.

[6] For Labienus cf. Sen. Rhet. *Controv.* X praef. 5–7 (who says that the author of the decree of the senate in this case lived to see his own books similarly burned); Suet. *Calig.* 16 (who states that Caligula revoked the ban upon these writings); for Cremutius Cordus cf. Suet. *l.c.*; Tac. *Ann.* IV 35 (who reports that this task fell to the aediles, but declares that secret copies escaped the flames and were in circulation); Dio Cass. LVII 24.3; for Cassius Severus cf. Suet. *l.c.* Cf. also Forbes, *op. cit.*, pp. 122–124; Sochatoff, *op. cit.*, p. 82. Dio Cass. LVI 27.1 says that Augustus ordered slanderous pamphlets about certain persons to be searched for and burned, in Rome by the aediles, in other places by the local officials, and that he punished some of the writers; cf. Forbes, *op. cit.*, p. 123.

NOTES ON BOOK-BURNING 147

Herennius Senecio respectively, described by Tacitus as *in comitio ac foro*.[7]

The curious circumstance has been remarked that trials for atheism and even for agnosticism appear in Greece, not in the more backward states, and neither in the more unsophisticated nor yet in the more servile ages, but at Athens, from about the beginning of the Peloponnesian War to the close of the fifth century.[8] Especially famous was the case against Protagoras, who was apparently one of the first to treat the existence of the gods as a debatable problem, which might on purely rational grounds [9] conceivably be solved in the negative,[10] since he stated at the beginning of his work on the gods: [11] "In regard to the gods I am not able to know either that they exist or that they do not exist, nor of what form they are, for there are many hindrances to knowledge, both the obscurity of the subject and the shortness of man's life." This assertion makes, by the repeated use of εἰδέναι, as Gomperz has pointed out, a clear distinction between *belief* and philosophical *knowledge*, yet the possible implications of such doubt were felt by his contemporary Athenians to be intolerable, so that he was condemned to exile and his books were burned in the agora — *in contione*,

---

[7] *Agr.* 2.1. Historical works were always exposed to the risk of destruction by those who found their statements of fact unreliable or unpalatable. In Cic. *De Div.* I 33 the expression *comburamus annales* is figurative, but may rest upon real foundations in fact.

[8] Cf. A. B. Drachmann, *Atheism in pagan Antiquity* (London, 1922), pp. 6–7; E. Derenne, *Les procès d'impiété* (Paris, 1930), p. 265; C. M. Bowra in *Class. Philol.* XXXIII (1938), 367.

[9] T. Gomperz, *Gr. Denker*, I⁴ (Berlin,1922), p. 493, quoting C. A. Lobeck.

[10] Drachmann, *op. cit.*, p. 42.

[11] H. Diels, *Vorsokratiker*, Protagoras B 4; most fully given by Eus. *Pr. Ev.* XIV 3.7; XIV 19.10; other cases include Plat. *Theaet.* 162d; Max. Tyr. 11.5; Diog. L.IX 51; Philostr. *Vit. Soph.* I 10; Epiphan. *Adv. Haer.* III 2.9; Lact. *Inst.* I 2.2; Schol. Plat. *Rep.* I 600 c(p. 273 Greene); Suid. s.v. Πρωταγόρας.

Cicero says.[12] The fires of religious intolerance there kindled have proved difficult to extinguish.

Diogenes Laertius [13] cites a statement by Aristoxenus in his *Historical Memoirs* that Plato — whether from professional jealousy, as Diogenes seems to imply, or from *odium theologicum* — wished to burn all the writings of Democritus that he could collect, but that Amyclas and Clinias the Pythagoreans prevented him, saying that there was no profit in so doing, since the books in question were already in wide circulation. In the case of Epicurus we have a most curious fragment of Aelian,[14] ingeniously (though not entirely convincingly) patched together by Hercher from several notices in Suidas,[15] which seems to read somewhat as follows: "And as he was sleeping, one of the priests [apparently of Asclepius] seemed to say to him that the one way to recovery for the man and the one remedy for the impending troubles was if he, burning the books of Epicurus, and kneading the ashes of these godless and impious and effeminizing letters (στιγμάτων) with moist wax, and making an application of this, should bind about the stomach and all the chest with bandages." To attempt to reason much about so uncertain a passage is unsafe; yet the medicinal use of the ash of particular substances — sometimes unusual, repulsive, or poisonous — is often mentioned. For example, a fragment of Cicero's *De Natura Deorum* preserved by Lactantius [16]

[12] Timon Phlias. ap. Sext. Emp. *Adv. Phys.* I 57; Cic. *N.D.* I 63; Val. Max. I 1, ext. 7 (Nepotianus); Diog. L. IX 52; Min. Fel. 8.3; Lact. *De Ira*, 9.1-2; Eus. *Pr. Ev.* XIV 19.10; Hier. *Chron.* ann. 1578 (cf. Syncell. p. 197); Schol. Plat. *Rep.* I 600c (p. 273 Greene); Suid. s.v. Πρωταγόρας. Since Protagoras was born *ca.* 484, and Plat. *Meno*, 91e says that he died when about seventy, his death would fall *ca.* 415, and his trial and exile — if the whole story be not a later invention, since Plato says that he died with undiminished reputation — might be dated a year or two earlier.
[13] IX 40.
[14] Fr. 89 Hercher.
[15] S. vv. ἀναδεύειν, καταδαρθάνειν, καταδεύσει, στίγματα, ταινίαι.
[16] *De Ira*, 13.12.

declares: "They say that a viper burned and reduced to ashes is a cure for the bite of the same beast," and Pliny [17] reports a similar theory about the ashes of the scorpion as a cure for its bite. I need not multiply instances, but merely suggest that the writings of Epicurus are perhaps here regarded as a sort of poison, which, like other venoms, may have its own curative properties. A clearer case affecting Epicurus is the statement of Lucian [18] that the peddler of oracles, Alexander of Abonuteichus in Paphlagonia, who felt his trade injured by Epicurus's denial of the possibility of divination, burned a volume of the Κύριαι Δόξαι of that author on a pile of fig-wood faggots in the market-place, "just as if he were burning the man in person, and threw the ashes into the sea, even adding an oracle as well:

> Burn with fire, I bid you, the doctrines of a purblind dotard."

According to some authorities, Diogenes Laertius [19] tells us, Arcesilaus revised and published certain works of his fellow Academic, Crantor, but according to others he burned them, the motive not being stated, save that we do learn from Diogenes that Crantor was a very voluminous writer while Arcesilaus himself left no writings,[20] from which we might perhaps infer that a difference in literary tastes rather than in philosophic views had prompted his action. In the burning by Bion the Borysthenite of the books of his former owner, a rhetorician,[21] there is probably no philosophic significance; but when Metrocles, after his

[17] *N.H.* XI 90.
[18] *Alex.* 47. Julian (*Letter to a Priest*, p. 301c — a passage called to my attention by Professor A. D. Nock) says of the discourses of Epicurus and Pyrrho that the gods have already in their wisdom destroyed their works, so that most of their books have ceased to be.
[19] IV 32.
[20] Diog. L. IV 24.
[21] Diog. L. IV 47.

conversion from the Peripatetic to the Cynic school, burned his notes of the lectures of Theophrastus,[22] the symbolism of the act is evident. Centuries later, in 212 A.D., Caracalla, whose hatred for the Aristotelians was due to his belief that Aristotle had been concerned in the death of Alexander the Great, whom he himself emulated, desired to burn the Peripatetic books, but there seems no evidence that he actually did so.[23]

Thus far the philosophers. The Greek religion seems not to have relied for defence upon book-burning, but at Rome, where church and state were rather closely connected, it was at times felt necessary, in order to protect both alike from subversive influences concealed under the cloak of religious books. In his description of the dangerous practices in 186 B.C., which prompted the famous *Senatus Consultum de Bacchanalibus*, Livy [24] makes the consul exclaim: "How often in the generation of our fathers and grandfathers has the duty been laid upon the magistrates that they should forbid the celebration of foreign rites, ban their sacrifices and soothsayers from the forum, circus, and city, seek out and burn their books of prophecies, and abolish all principles of sacrifice save those in accordance with the Roman ritual." The whole matter came to a head again five years later, in 181, in a famous incident described most fully by Pliny the Elder,[25] in a discussion of the antiquity of writing on papyrus. He says that Cassius Hemina (in the second century B.C.), in the fourth book of his annals, had stated that Cn. Terentius, a secretary, while digging in his garden on the Janiculum, had uncovered a chest in which King Numa had been buried. In it were found his books, written on *charta*, which was the more remarkable in that

[22] Diog. L. VI 95.
[23] Dio Cass. LXXVIII 7.3.
[24] XXXIX 16.8.
[25] *N.H.* XIII 84–88. Cf. W. W. Fowler, *The relig. Exp. of the Rom. People* (London, 1911), p. 349.

they had lasted so many years covered up in the ground. Hemina explained, however, that they had been carefully protected against decay by being enclosed in a hollow stone in the chest, completely sealed up with paraffine (*candelis*), and that in addition the books themselves had been fortified against worms by being treated with citrus-oil. In these books were writings of the Pythagorean philosophy, and because of their philosophic character they were burned by the praetor, Q. Petilius. Pliny further says that L. Calpurnius Piso, the annalist, said that these comprised seven books of pontifical law and the same number of Pythagorean volumes; C. Sempronius Tuditanus in his fourteenth book had asserted that they were books of the decrees of Numa; Varro, in book seven of his *Antiquitates humanae*, had mentioned twelve books; Valerius Antias in his second book had described twelve priestly books in Latin and twelve Greek books of philosophical precepts; in his third book he had said the same thing and also that it was decided that they should be burned. Augustine [26] quotes Varro in his book *De Cultu Deorum* for the circumstances of discovery, the vote of the senate, and the burning by the praetor, but gives his own explanation that Numa had, by illicit curiosity, learned certain secrets of the demons which he had noted down for his own use. These he was reluctant to impart to others, and so had had the note-books placed in his own tomb, which he thought would remain inviolate. The senate considered the books too dangerous to rebury, and in order to protect them from human curiosity decided on burning. Livy's account [27] describes two stone chests, eight by four feet each, with covers fastened on by lead; one was supposed to contain, as inscriptions indicated, the body of King Numa, the other his books. When the finder, at the advice of his friends, opened the one thought to contain the body, it was entirely empty; in the other two pack-

[26] *C.D.* VII 34.   [27] XL 29.3–14.

ages wrapped in paraffine contained seven books each, not only entire but very fresh in appearance (so far Livy's account suggests as source Cassius Hemina). Seven in Latin dealt with pontifical law; seven in Greek with philosophic theories such as might have been in vogue in Numa's time (a statement agreeing in part with that of Calpurnius Piso). Valerius Antias adds — here Livy discloses that his source was, in part, that notoriously unreliable annalist, though he does not agree with Pliny's statement that Antias mentioned two sets of twelve books each — that they were Pythagorean writings, and that there was a common tradition that Numa had been a pupil of Pythagoras — a view which Livy himself in I 18.2 had rejected as chronologically impossible. The books were read, at first by a few, then by others. The praetor urbanus, Q. Petilius, got a chance to read them, decided that they were subversive of religion (*pleraque dissolvendarum religionum esse*), and told the finder, L. Petilius, that he was going to burn them, giving him time first, however, to take legal action to recover possession of the books. The owner took the matter to the tribunes and they consulted the senate. The praetor declared that he was prepared to take oath that the books ought not to be read and preserved, and the senate, being satisfied with his statement, ordered that they be burned at the first opportunity, indemnifying the finder, however, for his loss. This indemnification he declined to accept, and the books were burned in the comitium, in the sight of the people, by the sacrificial attendants. Briefer but in close agreement with this account is that in Valerius Maximus.[28] Plutarch, in his life of Numa,[29] mentions the stone coffins, one for the body and the other with sacred books, written by Numa with his own hand, and quotes Antias for the twelve pontifical books and the twelve

[28] I 1.12.
[29] 22.1-5.

on Greek philosophy. The finding of the coffins was due, he says, to heavy rains about four hundred years after Numa's burial. No body was found, but the praetor, Petilius, told the senate that the writings ought not to be published, and they were accordingly burned in the comitium. The anonymous *De Viris illustribus* [30] refers very briefly to the story, and says that the books were burned *quia leves quasdam sacrorum causas continebant*. The account in Lactantius [31] has much in common with Livy, but says that by these philosophical books not merely the religious rites which Numa had himself instituted but also all others were jeopardized. Lactantius considers the burning a foolish performance, for what does it profit, he asks, that these books should be burned when this very fact is handed down to memory that the reason for their burning was because they undermined religious beliefs — a thought which might well have been pondered by some later suppressors of heretical doctrines.[32] One can but speculate what secrets these mysterious books may have contained — mere books on natural science have at later dates been exposed to destruction at the hands of those suspicious of *any* book — but it is tempting to recall Livy's statement [33] that Numa considered it important, in order to keep his rude subjects in a state of peace and justice, that the fear of the gods be inculcated in them, and hence devised his pretended noc-

[30] 3.2.
[31] *Inst*. I 22.5–8.
[32] From the proper names mentioned and the numbers and character of the books a rather interesting stemma of this tradition can be constructed, with Cassius Hemina, Sempronius Tuditanus, Calpurnius Piso, and Valerius Antias as the primary sources. Thus Varro, by his use of the number twelve, probably derives from Antias (and Augustine clearly from Varro), Livy continues the traditions of Hemina, Piso, and Antias (and is probably followed by Valerius Maximus and Lactantius), Pliny conflates five different sources, Plutarch quotes Antias, and the *De Viris illustribus* follows, directly or indirectly, Cassius Hemina.
[33] I 19.4–5. In what follows I thank Professor W. C. Greene for certain useful suggestions.

turnal conferences with the nymph Egeria. Now if these books – whose age was surely more nearly contemporary with the date of their discovery than with that of the second Roman king – rationalized the Roman and other religions as the products of fear inculcated for political and administrative purposes,[34] one can easily understand the motives for their suppression. This was an age at which skeptical works were beginning to appear at Rome, such as Ennius's *Euhemerus*, the exact date of which is unknown, though its *terminus ante quem* is the poet's death in 169, only a dozen years later than this discovery of Numa's books. The basic fact for our present inquiry is that these books were considered by the conservatives in power to be, because of their Greek and speculative character, a disintegrating influence upon the Roman religion – and through it upon the political system for which it furnished the sanction –, and hence as meriting destruction. The association of religious or philosophical cults with real or alleged political activities may be seen as early as the burning of the Pythagorean centre at Croton in the fifth century B.C., with the destruction of many of the members,[34a] and might thus have suggested the vigorous measures used in the case of these "Pythagorean" books.

Religious books might, however, be burned for other reasons. Varro's account, in his books of *Res divinae*, as reported by Lactantius,[35] of the way in which the Cumaean Sibyl offered Tarquinius Priscus nine books of prophecies for a certain price, burned three when he refused, and offered six for the same price, then burned three more, and finally sold him the remaining three at the price of the orig-

[34] Cf. the *Sisyphus* of Critias; also, later, Cicero, *N.D.* I 77.
[34a] Plut. *De Stoic. Repugn.* 37, p. 263c; Diog. L. VIII 39-40; other passages in G. Busolt, *Gr. Gesch.* II² (Gotha, 1895), p. 767, n. 2; p. 771, n. 3. On the incident cf. also J. Carcopino, *La basilique pythag. de la Porte Majeure* (1926), p. 185; T. Frank in *Class. Quart.* 21 (1927), 132.
[35] *Inst.* I 6. 10–11.

inal nine, is confirmed by other writers,[36] but in it there seems no general idea involved save that of a hard bargain, designed to increase the demand by diminishing the supply. Had the Sibyl, however, burned the last three books it might, in the long run, have been as well for the Roman people; in fact these volumes were actually burned in the conflagration which destroyed the Capitol on 6 July, 83 B.C.[37] At the command of the senate, however, a committee of three collected other Sibylline oracles in Italy and elsewhere to take the place of those burned,[38] but various unauthorized volumes continued to circulate, and in 12 B.C., when Augustus became Pontifex Maximus, he caused to be gathered and burned over two thousand anonymous or dubious works of prophetic writings, keeping only the Sibylline collection proper,[39] which was preserved in two gilded book-cases in the temple of Apollo on the Palatine, where they were consulted as late as the time of Maxentius,[40] only to be finally burned by Stilicho shortly after 400.[41]

The burning of magical books is occasionally mentioned, the most famous case being in the book of Acts,[42] where the practitioners of magic arts burned their books, valued at 50,000 pieces of silver. The life of *Barlaam and Ioasaph* [43] describes the similar act of the converted magician, Theu-

[36] Dion. Hal. IV 62.1–3; Plin. *N.H.* XIII 88 (who, like Solin. 2.17; Lyd. *De Mens*, IV 47; and Suid. s.v. 'Ηροφίλα, makes the number of the books three, two, and then one); App. *De Reg.* fr. 9 (ap. Bekk. *Anecd.* I 180); Zonar. VII 11 (who notes both traditions as to the numbers, three reduced to one or nine reduced to three).
[37] Plut. *Sull.* 27.6; App. *B.C.* I 86; Plin. *N.H.* XIII 88; Tac. *Ann.* VI 12.4; *Hist.* III 72.
[38] Varr. ap. Dion. Hal. IV 62.6; Tac. *Ann.* VI 12.1–5.
[39] Suet. *Aug.* 31.1.
[40] [Lact.] *De Mort. Pers.* 44.8; Zosim. II 16.1. Certain allusions in Claudian (*e.g., De Bell. Gild.* I 29–30) are rather indefinite.
[41] Rutil. II 51–52 (and Vessereau's note on p. 308).
[42] 19.19; and see the learned note of J. J. Wetstein *ad loc.*
[43] 32.302. See also the burning of magical books mentioned by Greg. Naz. *Or.* 24.12 (*Patr. Gr.* XXXV, 1184a).

das, and in the fourth century the books of Bishop Paulinus of Dacia, who was accused of dabbling in magic, were burned by a fellow-bishop.[44] Under Valens action taken against magical books was so vigorous that in the Orient owners of books, through fear of a like fate, burned their entire libraries.[45]

In the Jewish-Christian tradition in its relations to paganism book-burnings were frequent, but I shall here mention only a few of the earlier cases. In 168 B.C. Antiochus Epiphanes, in his attacks upon the Jews, had the books of the Law torn in pieces and burned,[46] and similar action by a Roman soldier in the middle of the first century after Christ is recorded by Josephus.[47] In the great persecution of the Christians by Diocletian in 303 the burning of Gospels, Bibles, and other sacred books is mentioned, especially in Africa and Spain,[48] and the feeling that those who had surrendered their sacred books for destruction had proved themselves traitors to the Christian faith appears prominently in the contentions made by the Donatist heretics against the orthodox.[49] Arnobius asserts that it would have been more in the interest of the pagan religion had the pagans burned some of their own unchaste and shameful books and

---

[44] Hilar. *Op. hist.* fr. 3.27 (*Patr. Lat.* X, 674). For later times cf. Shakesp. *Tempest*, III 2.99–105 (and H. H. Furness *ad loc.*); Cervantes, *Don Quixote*, ch. 6; H. C. Lea, *Hist. of the Inquisition*, III (1888), 446; 453; 490.

[45] Amm. Marc. XXIX 2.4.

[46] I Macc. 1.56; Sulp. Sev. *Chron.* II 19.8: *sacra etiam legis et prophetarum volumina igni cremata.*

[47] *Bell. Iud.* II 229.

[48] The passages are collected by Forbes, *op. cit.*, pp. 120–121; to which add [Lact.] *De Mort. Persec.* 12.2; Aug. *De Bapt.* V 1; Geoff. of Monmouth, V 5; Gildas, *Hist.* 9. Suid. s.v. Διοκλητιανός says that Egyptian books of alchemy were also burned, to keep that race from reserves of wealth which might prompt resistance to the Romans. It is not quite clear to just which persecution Hier. *In Zach.* II, p. 841 Vall. refers, though Forbes (p. 120, n. 23) connects the allusion with this one.

[49] Cf. Aug. *C. Donat. Ep.* 48; *Ep.* 185.30; *C. Crescon.* III 80–81; IV 10.

NOTES ON BOOK-BURNING 157

shut up their demoralizing theatres,[50] while as for the influence of the Christian books, they were, he maintained, far less destructive of religious beliefs than were the theological works of Cicero.[51]

I find no clear indication that Julian, despite all the charges laid at his door, was guilty of the burning of Christian books, though one of his letters,[52] to the prefect of Egypt, expresses a wish that such might be annihilated. But after his death his Christian successor Jovian burned the pagan library which Julian had founded at Antioch,[53] in 371 Valens, in torturing the people of that city, burned many of their books (though most of them were concerned with the arts and jurisprudence),[54] and in the next century (448 A.D.) the anti-Christian writings of Porphyry were consigned to the flames,[55] which seems to have been about the last such action taken by Christians against pagan works, though this method, which had been used in the time of Constantine against the books of Arius,[56] continued to be frequently employed against heretical writings.[57] Lake and Cadbury[58] remark that the adoption of this device by

[50] IV 36.
[51] III 7. The curious prophetic passage in Lact. *Inst.* VII 17.8 which declares that an evil king arising in Syria *iustos homines obvolvet libris prophetarum atque ita cremabit*, possibly illustrates this form of hostility toward religious books, but suggests the *tunica molesta* (Schol. Juv. 8.235), and otherwise has little to teach us about historic facts.
[52] *Ep.* 23, p. 378b.
[53] Suid. s.v. 'Ιοβιανός; Ioann. Antioch. fr. 181 (*F. H. G.* IV, p. 607).
[54] Amm. Marc. XXIX 1.41.
[55] *Cod. Iustin.* I 1.3 (cf. *Cod. Theod.* XVI 5.66); *Sacr. Concil.... Collectio*, V, 1761, p. 417 b–c Mansi. Marcus Diaconus, *Vita S. Porphyrii* 71 – called to my notice by Professor A. D. Nock –, describes the burning of pagan books, as well as of pagan images, at Gaza in 402.
[56] Soc. *H.E.* I 8 (*Patr. Gr.* LXVII, p. 64c). Note also Rufin. *H.E.* I 2 for the burning by the Emperor at the Council of Nicaea of *libelli* of complaints lodged with him by various bishops against one another.
[57] Cf. Forbes, *op. cit.*, p. 122 for several cases.
[58] In F. J. F. Jackson and K. Lake, *The Beginnings of Christianity* (London, 1933), IV, 243.

Christian theologians probably explains the loss of the Greek text of Tatian's *Diatessaron*,[59] of many works of Origen, and of most Gnostic and other heretical works. The long story of such later burnings within the Christian fold itself, like that of conflagrations for political reasons, lies outside the time limits of the present discussion. Interesting, however, is the tradition recounted by the Christian writer Bar Hebraeus (Abulfaragius) [60] that when Alexandria was captured in 640 and the Peripatetic philosopher John the Grammarian attempted, through the offices of the Arab general 'Amr, to persuade the caliph Omar to save the famous Alexandrian library, Omar replied that if the books in it agreed with the Koran they were superfluous, but if they disagreed they were heretical, therefore in either case the library should be burned. Accordingly the books were distributed as fuel to the public baths of the city. This story, though repeated by many writers, is to be regarded as a picturesque fiction.[61]

In conclusion some suggestions as to possible reasons for the choice of this method of destruction may be advanced. First and most obvious, this is, as distinguished from erasing, tearing, burying, or throwing into water, an absolutely thorough and irreparable act. Secondly, it lends itself better than other forms to conspicuous, public, communal expressions of condemnation. These two reasons are perhaps adequate, yet I cannot escape the feeling that two others also had some effect, namely, third, the purifying power of

---

[59] To be sure, a fragment of the Greek has been found at Dura, perhaps dating from Tatian's own time; cf. C. Hopkins in *Am. Journ. of Arch.* XXXVII (1933), 473.

[60] See the references in J. B. Bury's edition of E. Gibbon, *Decline and Fall of the Rom. Emp.* V (1914), p. 482.

[61] Cf. Gibbon, *l.c.*; W. Muir, *The Caliphate* [revised by T. H. Weir, (1924)], p. 166; R. Guest in *The Encycl. of Islam* (London, 1927), II 537. On the burning of public libraries at Byzantium cf. Suid. s.v. Μάλχος; K. Dziatzko in P.-W. III (1899), 420.

fire, which was widely recognized,[62] and which would, in the case of books of a polluting or blasphemous character, be highly appropriate; and, fourthly, in certain of the earlier cases, as in that of Protagoras, for example, the burning of a man's book — that is, of the expression of his words and thought — may have been supposed, by a principle of sympathetic (or even, perhaps, of contagious) magic, to have affected the guilty one himself, as in other cases of the magical treatment of objects closely associated with him. That this last reason is not entirely absent may be judged from the case in Lucian's *Alexander* [63] already cited, where Alexander publicly burned the Κύριαι Δόξαι of Epicurus on faggots of fig-wood, *just as if he were burning the man in person*, that is, making the book act in lieu of an effigy.[64] Of course I should not assert that this magical notion is found in all, or even in most, cases of book-burning, but as a primitive and residual cause it may have had a larger part than we might at first thought suppose.

That the frequent result of such burnings, particularly when publicly performed, was to advertise rather than to exterminate the volumes in question may be illustrated from the statement of Tacitus [65] that when certain abusive books by the informer Veiento had been burned at the order of Nero, "so long as they were only to be procured at a risk they were sought out and repeatedly read, but when it later became permissible to own them they fell into oblivion." Dio Cassius [66] remarks that the interest of the public in the works of Cremutius Cordus, when they were eventually republished, from concealed copies, after suppression by burning, was all the greater. A similar conclu-

[62] Cf. Virg. *Aen.* VI 742: *infectum eluitur scelus aut exuritur igni.*
[63] 47.
[64] On the burning of effigies see, for example, J. G. Frazer, *The Golden Bough* 3 (London, 1917), I, 55–78; X (1914), 106–130; 159.
[65] *Ann.* XIV 50.
[66] LVII 24.4.

sion may be drawn from a striking case in Chinese history.[67] In 213 B.C. there occurred in China a famous burning of literary, historical, and philosophical books, exceptions being made in favor of works on medicine, pharmacy, agriculture, and divination, and also of the private libraries of a group of "scholars of wide learning." This was done at the order of the Grand Councillor, Li Ssŭ, ostensibly to prevent the invoking of records of a golden past in order to disparage contemporary society and government. Yet a little later, in the Han dynasty, many of these destroyed classics were restored, as well as was then possible, from oral tradition, and the practical result was to develop in China a cult of books and to strengthen the backward-looking psychology of the Chinese people, thereby completely defeating the intention of Li Ssŭ.[68] That the results of many later burnings have been similar to this case there seems little reason to doubt, and the wide dispersal of books since the invention of printing has tended to reduce such acts to annoying, insulting, or ridiculous gestures rather than effective agencies for the suppression of unwelcome ideas.

F. H. Cramer's article on "Bookburning and Censorship in ancient Rome" (*Journ. of the Hist. of Ideas*, 6 [1945], 157-196) came to my notice too late to be used in this paper, but well deserves mention here.

[67] I am indebted to my colleagues, Professors W. E. Clark and J. R. Ware for the reference in the following note.
[68] D. Bodde, *China's first Unifier*, etc., in *Sinica Leidensia* (Leiden, 1938), III, 22-24; 80-84; 162-166.

RELIGION AND POETRY

Frederick Clifton Grant
Union Theological Seminary

The assertion is often made — I do not know who made it first — that more people would accept the Church's creeds if they were always sung, never said. It would be interesting to know what prompts this assertion. Does it imply that people would then not take the creeds so seriously, just as they will sing any words that happen to be set to familiar or attractive music? Would the creeds thus be reduced to the level of most hymns, which apparently can be sung without ever thinking of their meaning? — especially when muffled in the swathing bands of sentimental mellifluity, music as meaningless as the jingle of their words. Or does the statement involve a genuinely philosophical or even religious appraisal of the creeds? They are affirmations of faith; and the proper setting for the profoundest affirmations of faith is surely public worship. "We believe in one God, the Pantocrator, Maker of heaven and earth, and of all things visible and invisible"; and we say this, conscious of the fact that we are in the very presence of the God in whom we believe. "And in Jesus Christ, his only Son, our Lord" — the mystery of whose Incarnation, whose redemption, whose death, resurrection and exaltation we are even now engaged in celebrating. Here is the proper atmosphere of the creed; here *lex orandi* and *lex credendi* are one.

If this is the meaning of the claim which I have quoted, then no doubt many of us will be inclined to assent, even though, historically, it was a long time before the Church put her creeds to music. Indeed it was a long time before the creeds were introduced into public worship at all — in the west, not until the sixth century, and in Rome not until 1014, when the creed was used in the midnight mass at Christmas. The use of musical settings for the creeds was presumably later still. The musical history of the early church is the record of considerable conservatism. As St. Jerome insisted, "David is our Simonides, our Pindar and our Alcaeus," and the Psalter provided the music of the Eucharist as well as of other services, up at least to the time of Jerome. It was sung, presumably, to the same austere tunes or chants that the Jews had used from the days of the second temple; the introduction of Greek modes was late, and tentative, and met no little opposition. One recalls the comments of St. Augustine, in his *Confessions*, upon the introduction of the new modes by St. Ambrose at Milan. The early Church was too puritan, too restrained, too serious, during the age of the martyrs and for a century after the triumph under Constantine, to indulge in what must have seemed to many persons dangerously worldly elaborations of public worship. The pagans used such music, especially the Phrygian votaries of the Great Mother and Attis, with their shrill flutes; that made Greek music suspect, for sober-minded Christians. And it had heretical associations as well; the Arians, it was said, filled the barber shops of Alexandria with their tunes. To adopt — or even adapt — such music to the sacred purposes of worship seemed a daring innovation, almost like the modern Salvation Army's use of popular tunes, as settings for pious words, in their street services. Nevertheless, the experiment was made. Then came the Gregorian chant, and the whole miraculous efflorescence of Christian hymnody and song, through the centuries of the Middle Ages, and later, and down to our own time. Even the sternest of modern puritans would not think of banishing all music save psalm-chants from worship — while the English Puritans, in the seventeenth century, were represented by some of the best hymn writers of the time.

Nevertheless, something has come over the Christian religion since the close of the Middle Ages, something not limited to the use of music in worship, or the kind of music used. For example, hymns are now more subjective in tone than were those of earlier periods. The change is one that affects our whole approach to religion, our whole attitude to and thought about it, our whole conception of religious truth; and the music used in public worship is only one aspect of this change. On the whole there has been *a decline of poetry in religion*, or of religious poetry — and this reflects a totally different orientation of religious thought from the one in which Christianity was cradled, and which for ten centuries and more was the natural expression of its most characteristic ethos. We can see the change beginning to come about as scholasticism became entrenched in Western theology: the Eucharistic controversies were the harbinger of the dark dawn; then came the fully recovered Aristotle in the early thirteenth century; then the High Scholasticism of Thomas and his contemporaries and successors; finally arose the Reformation theologies, Calvinism, the Counter-Reformation, Trent, and the whole modern idea that theology is a science, and may be set forth *more geometrico*, with absolute logic and irrefutable proofs. It suited the age of growing physical science to find religious faith capable of expression in scientific formulae, convincing to the reason, and demonstrable to Jew, Moslem, and pagan, as well as to the Christian believer with his special Spirit-guided experience. Of course, there has been plenty of religious poetry since the sixteenth century; moreover, the architectonic formulation of Christian faith was not only the result of the growing scientific spirit in the Western world; it also came from the innate demand for clarity of thought — something that also lies behind, and antedates, modern Western science, as Whitehead has shown. Another qualification to be made is the coexistence of mysticism along with — and even within — the rigid theological systems of the Reformation and Counter-Reformation; perhaps Lutheranism was somewhat more congenial to it than were other systems, though Anglicanism has certainly always been friendly to the mystical tendency. Moreover, science, and scientific theology, themselves contain a poetic element; but this is not often apparent, except in the works of the very greatest scientific minds of the past and present.

In view of all these inevitable qualifications, perhaps our thesis should be restated: something has come over the Christian religion, during recent centuries, to make poetry *less at home* in the Christian fold; to substitute formal, logical statements of theology for the ardent, inspired, imaginative expression of faith in objective eternal realities; to make the personal or individual apprehension of truth and experience of salvation the subject-matter of poetic creation, thus narrowing its field intolerably and giving the impression that faith is purely and simply what this person or that thinks about life, instead of the full rushing tide of a new life which has come into the world, and the social response of a vast group to this transforming event. Christian poetry has become — with many exceptions, it is true — the versified private philosophy of A, B, or C, rather than the song of the redeemed — "the redeemed" of course being written, as in earlier ages, in the plural. This change, as far as it has already taken place, means a great loss to religion, rather than any gain.

Of course there have been counter-movements, both hymnological and liturgical, and also protests, and efforts to regain lost ground. One of these is clearly reflected in our new Church Hymnal of the Episcopal Church: *The Hymnal 1940*, with its wealth of older hymns, celebrating the objective realities toward which normal Christian worship is always orientated. Other recent hymnals, in other

RELIGION AND POETRY

parts of the Christian Church, afford similar evidence of a widespread attempt to get back to sounder principles. The Liturgical Movement might be cited as further proof. But we still have a long way to go.

Perhaps I can illustrate the difference between the modern and the ancient in religious poetry by using the quotations that Sir Richard Livingstone has chosen for the purpose of showing the contrast between modern poetry and classical (*The Greek Genius*, p. 41). Classic poetry, he says, "gives the text, the modern expounds it. The classic shows us the scene, the modern explains what feelings it should evoke. Indeed, the modern is sometimes so bent on this, that he fails to ensure that we shall actually see the scene itself. It is so, in this description of the declining year:

> In the mid-days of autumn, on their eves
> The breath of Winter comes from far away,
> And the sick west continually bereaves
> Of some gold tinge, and plays a roundelay
> Of death among the bushes and the leaves.

Keats suggests to us the sighing winds, the faded colours, the melancholy atmosphere of autumnal decay, but he brings nothing definite before our senses: unlike Tennyson who, writing in the classical manner, makes us both to see and hear

> Through the faded leaf
> The chestnut pattering to the ground."

The parallels, in Christian hymnody, are not difficult to draw! As against the subjectivism of much modern religious poetry, or even of such precious, and would-be objective, hymns as Isaac Watts's famous one,

> When I survey the wondrous cross
>   Where the young Prince of Glory died,
> My richest gain I count but loss,
>   And pour contempt on all my pride —

contrast the stately objectivity of the ancient hymns, for example the *Pange Lingua* of Venantius Fortunatus:

> Sing, my tongue, the glorious battle,
> Sing the winning of the fray;
> Now above the cross, the trophy,
> Sound the high triumphal lay:
> Tell how Christ, the world's Redeemer,
> As a victim won the day.

The whole hymn (not one of the best, but representative) describes the scene, but it does not tell us how to feel about it — not even how its author feels about it; but you can hardly sing that hymn *without* feeling what you should, *i.e.*, what all Christians have always felt as they "came upon the Figure crucified," and saw Christ's passion once more "placarded before their eyes." The difference is, the older hymn centers our interest in Christ, while the more modern centers *its* interest in the believer; with the consequence that if anyone cannot sing the words with intense devotion he either gives up entirely, or sings with a lurking sense of unreality, even of hypocrisy. One is an evangelical proclamation of the fact of redemption; the other is a rhymed exhortation, addressed to the people in the pews — in brief, a sermon in verse. And the extraordinary thing about the whole contrast is that the modern, subjective, homiletical hymn is usually thought to be "evangelical"; whereas the truth is surely that the clear, classic, objective statement of fact, depicting of scene, or narrative of event, is much closer to the manner of the Gospels and to their method of presenting the Christian faith. Even when the old hymns indulge in rhetorical purple, or wander off into realms of fancy, as in Fortunatus's lines,

> Sweetest wood, and sweetest iron!
> Sweetest weight is hung on thee,

it is still the "tree," not my feelings, that the hymn is concerned about.

RELIGION AND POETRY 167

Or take some of the more sugary and scarcely classical elaborations in the breviary — as where St. Helena finds the true cross and St. Benedict destroys the pot of poison by the sign of the cross, and with three stones brings up a fountain of water on the mountain-top; where St. Peter twice rescues St. Paul from shipwreck, and St. Lawrence the Deacon opens the eyes of the blind; where Blessed Mary ascends her starry throne amid the blessing of the angels, while her fragrant name lingers among mortals "like unto cinnamon, and as aspalathus, and yielding a pleasant odor like the best myrrh." The best myrrh! *We* do not know one kind from another! And what in the world is aspalathus? The fragrant tree, no doubt, beloved of the young unicorn! (Though see Ecclus. 24:15, the praise of Wisdom.) We are in a strange wonder-world, a world of fancies and dreams, of mystical and allegorical lore, of miracles and marvels, where our two best guides are the *Golden Legend* and the *Acta Sanctorum*. It is a world of poetry — the authors of the Homeric Hymns would have appreciated this lore, and would have compared aspalathus with that magic flower — the narcissus — beloved by gods and men, which Korê was reaching out to pluck when "the Host of Many" seized her and carried her off to his gloomy halls. It is a world of poetry and of imagination we have entered. True, it may be rather poor poetry, very post-classical and not up to the glorious heights of such hymns as *Conditor alme siderum*, or *Verbum supernum prodiens* — but it is poetry, nevertheless; undeniably and unquestionably it is poetry. The change I am speaking of might be illustrated from the different appreciation of biblical metaphors in, let us say, Ruskin's *Modern Painters*, volume I of which appeared in 1843, a century ago, and in Somerset Maugham's autobiographic *Summing Up*, where the influence of the Bible upon English literature is wholly deprecated. Ruskin becomes eloquent in describing the biblical metaphors — the sky represented as a tabernacle, or God as "laying His beams in the waters" — while Somerset Maugham on the other hand holds that the influence of the Bible upon English literature has been very detrimental, since it has popularized vague, cloudy, incomprehensible figures of speech whose real meaning no one can quite understand but only vaguely feel. Certainly a change has come over the "reading public" in a hundred years.

I think, sometimes, that our current religious education and also our current preaching likewise reflect the change that has come over the modern world. Too much of both is concerned with the subject, "How should we feel about this and that," not enough with the subject, "What hath God wrought!" Indeed, the treacherous word "feel" has now usurped a large area that properly belongs to "think" and "will." I had a good illustration of this not long ago. After a radio broadcast I handed in a question to the speaker: "If the mandated Pacific islands are to be returned to Japan after the war, how do you propose to prevent another Japanese war of aggression, using them for bases?" But the question was revised by a young lady, a journalism-major, whose duty it was to turn all submitted questions into proper English, and so it ran, "How would you *feel* that we should proceed, in trying to prevent another war in the Pacific?" I must say that I for one did not feel especially pacific, when I heard the revised question read out!

Take the story of Joseph, in the Book of Genesis — one of the most beautiful examples of prose-poetry in all the world. Suppose we are to use it in the Church School or in the pulpit as an example of forgiveness. There is surely feeling enough in it! "Then Joseph could not refrain himself before all them that stood by him; and he cried, Cause every man to go out from me. And there stood no man with him, while Joseph made himself known unto his brethren. And he wept aloud: and the Egyptians heard, and the house of Pharaoh heard. And Joseph said unto his brethren, I am Joseph; doth my father yet live? And his brethren could not answer him; for they were troubled at his presence." That is magnificently told; but the point is not what Joseph *felt*, or the brethren; the point is the equally simple statement that follows: "I am Joseph your brother, whom ye sold into Egypt. And now be not grieved, nor angry with yourselves, that ye sold me hither: for God did send me before you to preserve life." There is the point of the story, as the Psalmist saw:

> He sent a man before them;
> Joseph was sold for a servant. (105:17.)

It is not how we should feel forgiveness — but how forgiveness is a necessary, inevitable step in a process which God has devised, which God overrules, which God uses in the working-out of his purposes. All the pathos, the tragedy, the triumph in this story centers there — the theme is one which Homer could have used, or Sophocles, for "God was working his purpose out," mysteriously, inexorably, through the tangled mazes of human behavior and the apparently adventitious events of one man's life: Διὸς δ' ἐτελείετο βουλή. You cannot really *teach* that lesson; it has to be absorbed, drunk in, like all poetry; and I fancy a boy reading that tale in the attic on a rainy Sunday afternoon will find more in it than any "lesson" in a church school textbook could ever convey, or than any amount of homiletical paraphrase from the pulpit could awaken in his mind. It teaches by indirection, and by objectivity, and without saying a word about how anyone should feel or behave. And from it a boy can learn more about the normal and the abnormal motivation of human life than from a dozen contemporary scenes dressed up as projects or problems, all about Johnny and Henry and Tommy.

The same is true in the gospels. Jesus' teaching is in

poetic form. He tells stories — "parables," we call them, because they laid some tale or event from human experience or observation side by side with the divine truth or the principle of action which he was expounding — though, as always, men tended to remember the story and forget which truth it illustrated; so that we have only the vague clue, "The Kingdom of heaven is like" this or that. Even his didactic teaching was in poetic form, as has often been observed. But the gospel writers do not simply hand on a book of teaching — it is the life of Jesus that interests them, and us. The saying in the Sermon on the Mount is no doubt poetic in form:

> Love your enemies,
> And pray for them that persecute you;
> That ye may be sons of your Father
> > who is in heaven:
> For he maketh his sun to rise
> > on the evil and the good,
> And sendeth rain
> > on the just and the unjust.

But it is not simply his didactic teaching that conveys this lesson. It is the whole spirit of the Lord, which makes the profoundest impression — as in Luke's Passion Narrative, where he quite obviously *substitutes* for Mark's cry of dereliction that final word from the cross, "Father, into thy hands I commend my spirit," but precedes it with that other word, "Father, forgive them; for they know not what they do." It is this utterance from the cross, which Carlyle called "the sublimest word ever uttered," that has touched the hearts of men, and has made divine forgiveness the very key to the understanding of the Gospel, for countless millions of people, Christian and non-Christian. Now it is poetry that has given us this interpretation — Luke's gospel is a superb example of what Norden called *die antike Kunstprosa*. The full bearings of that interpretation have not yet been taken, though W. L. Knox, in his recent Schweich Lectures on *Some Hellenistic Elements in Primitive Christianity*, has advanced the study a further stage. Luke is *not* a historian, in our modern sense; no writer in the ancient world was a modern historian, not even Thucydides, who probably comes nearest being one. History was an art, allied to rhetoric; and the books that set forth religious truth in narrative form were often poetic, *i.e.*, dramatic; the days of the religious romance, of Apuleius and Philostratus, were still in the future. And for a writer steeped as thoroughly in the Old Testament as Luke was, the dramatic presentation of the essential, timeless, divine truth was far more important than any stenographic record or chronicle of bare events could possibly be. We recognize, as a rule, the importance of this principle in reading the Gospel of John; but it is also true of the Synoptics. How otherwise are we to account for Luke's, and even Matthew's, plain refusal to take over some of the Marcan sayings, *e.g.*, Luke's detour about Mark 10:45 or 16:7? The sovereign freedom with which later evangelists revise the work of the earlier — suggesting that Mark perhaps did the same with his sources — can be explained only on the assumption that they are not writing history or biography, as we understand history and biography, but something else — I venture to think of it as something at least akin to what a poet does in reshaping a story in order to bring out its meaning more clearly or more effectively. This principle of interpretation does not do away with "the historical element in the gospels," of course — but allows us to view it more fairly, recognizing that neither Jewish or Jewish-Christian tradition nor Hellenistic Greek evangelists had the slightest idea of what our age would be looking for, *viz.*, scientific history; or would have been concerned to meet our requirements had they known them. This approach may help us to understand such passages as the Temptation narrative or the scene in the Garden of Gethsemane, where no human reporter was present. These scenes are "in character," and true, but they are surely poetic, *i.e.*, the product of creative imagination, not of stenographic reporting.

Poetry is more philosophical than history (Aristotle *Poetics* 1451b). The recognition of this distinction would help us a long way in the interpretation of the Bible, and also of the creeds; it would make modernism unnecessary, and it might cure us of the peculiar woodenness and dogmatism of much current (and even ancient) orthodoxy. For we should then realize that poetry, which aims to express the ineffable, to convey what passes beyond the logical understanding, which makes use of symbols — not only for the conveying of facts, but also for conveying spiritual states, inner realities beyond the range of direct description — we would realize that poetry itself is not to be interpreted as prose, as arithmetic, geology, botany, topography or history, but only as something superior to them all and *sui generis*. It is akin to what we vaguely call "mysticism," and makes use of symbols — not only using symbols for facts but even symbols of symbols, so that there results a hierarchy of meanings, and "each truth is symbol, save the last." Such things cannot be scientifically demonstrated: they can never be proved, only apprehended. Half the energies of certain writers on systematic theology have been wasted, in the past, for they endeavored to understand, explain, and correlate as prosaic statements of fact what are inevitably poetic terms or metaphors for truths that can never be handled that way — never, at any rate, with such intellects as we possess, geared as they are to external realities and produced, as Bergson held, in conflict with the natural physical order.

Take St. Paul's great metaphors of salvation: redemption from slavery, adoption as sons, rebirth, mystical union with Christ, sacrifice and atonement — he never dreamed of putting these in a series, as successive stages in salvation. But that is what some of the older systematic writers tried to do. Or take the cross: how, and why, and with what presuppositions in the mind of God, the cross should be the turning point in the world's relation to God, and the crux, literally, in the salvation of men, no biblical writer even attempts to say. The great overwhelming fact of salvation, and the consequent new life in Christ, new relation to God — this is what the cross symbolized, but never explained. It is *not* "preaching the cross" to ignore all this, and talk as if there were no mystery about it, nothing obscure and profound and totally beyond our comprehension in this inconceivable, unhoped for act of divine goodness and grace. The cross is purest poetry: it is the undreamt, unanticipated, divine denouement which comes at the end of the darkest human tragedy, and at the same time it is the "revelation of the mystery" hid from the beginning of time, and the fresh start of the "new creation" by God. To lose sight of all this results in the cheap, familiar clap-trap of much modern "preaching of the cross," some of it in revivalist tabernacles and over the radio, some of it, alas, in solemn Three Hours services on Good Friday.

Or take the miracle stories in the gospels. The rationalism that would explain the Feeding of the Multitude as a lakeside picnic, or the Walking on the Water as a lonely stroll of Jesus along the beach, while his disciples labored at their oars out on the lake, or the Stilling of the Tempest as Jesus' rebuke of the disciples' fears, or even Peter's Stater found in the fish's mouth as the proceeds of the sale of the fish (quite a fish, to sell for two drachmas!) — all this is lumbering, pedantic, obtuse, nineteenth century nonsense. (Ponderous Teutonic nonsense, much of it.) You cannot interpret these stories that way, and keep them alive; they are like flowers which are pulled apart, petal by petal, and can never regain their pristine freshness and beauty. But by the same token, an interpretation that aims to keep them as *fact*, as literal accounts of what actually happened, ignoring the human element of tradition and the growth of legend, and also ignoring the boundless faith that either created or conditioned them (*i.e.*, without which they never could have occurred) — that is just as crude, just as heavy and lumbering, just as stupid and deadly as the old rationalist interpretations, however pious its intention or orthodox its language.

The best example is the Lucan Infancy Narrative. Here we have the purest prose poetry in the whole New Testament. The stories here woven together make up "the Lucan Idyl," as the term is used. The sources may be tradition, with a certain amount of legendary accretion; a strong element of Old Testament story and language is present — as the black-face type in Nestle and WH makes clear; there may be some influence from Hellenistic Jewish sources (Dibelius points out in his *Jungfrauensohn* the parallels in Philo); but such considerations do not take us to the heart of the story. It must be read as poetry — and enjoyed, as a child enjoys the Christmas story — to be fully appreciated and apprehended. We must read it as we read an idyl of Theocritus — a perfect sketch of a *scene*, *e.g.*, the Harvest Home, or the Country Singing Matches, to compare slight things with serious; or the equally idyllic and far more closely relevant tale of Samuel's childhood in the Old Testament, or the story of Joseph, or the 'Idyl' of Ruth or that of Judith — these short stories provide much closer parallels. But, someone will ask, are these tales *true*? Of course — but not in the sense of a stenographic record of everything that was said, or the reporter's notebook of events, or the next day's newspaper account of whatever transpired. They are true *as poetry* — which is more true, at least more true philosophically, than the annals of history. The truth of the Lucan Idyl is the picture it gives of the life of humble,

RELIGION AND POETRY

simple piety which was the best thing in the world, certainly in Judaism, in its time, and indispensable for the background of the Gospel which Luke is writing — indispensable, too, for an understanding of that Gospel, or of the life of Jesus, or his teaching, or the rise of the Christian religion. Which is the truer, Herodotus' picturesque prose account of the Persian War, or Aeschylus' vivid drama? Fortunately, we do not have to choose between them! The poet does not relate facts, or does so only incidentally; but he makes the motives real, and gives us the feeling of the situation, the tension, the strain, the terror, the triumph, the mourning, even the pity and the tragedy of the defeated. Prose narrative cannot do that — except by taking the wings of the imagination, moving into a new dimension, and itself becoming in some degree poetry.

It is not a question of poetry, or legend, *versus* history: instead, it is poetry *versus* the abstract ideal of scientific stenographically reported history, the ancient *art* of history *versus* the modern *science* of history. The question of historicity is not ignored, but it does not come first; what comes first is a consideration of the methods by which the accounts of the past have been transmitted, whether by tradition, by legend, by poetic narrative, or by hard and fast factual record. The biblical history, from first to last, belongs to the former type rather than the latter.

Or take the Creeds. There is not a phrase in them which is not poetic, except perhaps the appositional clause, "he was crucified, dead, and buried." God is not "the Father," save as that word is used to convey a relation faintly suggested by human fatherhood; nor is he "Almighty" or "All-ruling" or "Sovereign," save in a sense that leaves our conceptions of Omnipotence, the sum total of power, far behind; nor is he "Maker of heaven and earth," though the truth behind and beyond those words lies in the direction toward which they point, but far beyond them — as we say "the sun *shines*," though that is only a very mild word for the sun's inconceivable energies and luminous, life-giving power. These familiar terms are all wrapped in mystery, and the truth they set forth can never be more than faintly suggested, never fully conveyed, never proved, by their use — or even by their fuller interpretation; for the truth behind them must be apprehended by the believer himself, not by a process of logical inference, or by exegesis, philological or historical, but immediately, as his own act of faith. And on beyond these words lie the tremendous affirmations of the Christological section: "One Lord, Jesus Christ; begotten, not made; of one substance with the Father; God from God; Light from Light; true God from true God; who for us men and for our salvation came down from heaven, and was made man." Of course these words should be sung! They are the very heart of Christian doctrine, as set forth in the New Testament and in all orthodox theology. But they are poetry, purest poetry, and can never be proved, like scientific formulas or historical statements or other prosaic records of fact. Their truth lies on beyond the range of historical or factual demonstration, though in the same direction as our grasp of the general meaning of history leads us to follow; and the full apprehension of that truth involves imagination on our part, *i.e.*, a poetic quality in us akin to that which produced this transcendent terminology, and it also involves a set of the will, the "leap" of faith, the submission of ourselves to the full consequences of that apprehension, once it is made. It is the veriest axiom of the Christian life that the "pure in heart" see God, rather than the profound, or the clever, or the learned, or even the valiant. For the pure in heart yield themselves to nothing else, and so have no mixed motives to disentangle. That must be what our Lord meant when he commended children, as close to God's Kingdom: they give themselves without reserve, in utter response, to what is apprehensible by the imagination, rather than demanding proof, signs, evidences, that dull species of "unfaith clamoring to be coined to faith by proof."

Of course, all this will be misinterpreted, if one assumes that "poetry" means either limericks or purely imaginary narrative or discourse, or the cultivated obscurity of current faddists; or that "fiction" means detective stories, murder mysteries, or twenty-five-cent thrillers. But poetry is no external decoration added to life; it wells up out of its very heart — that is, the *great* poetry does, Homer, Sophocles, Shakespeare, Keats, Dante. This, the true poetry, is more "philosophical," more illuminating, than much that passes for "history," *i.e.*, the hard, cold, factual record of events.

What we need most of all in our modern religion, I believe, is (a) a revival of true poetry, and (b) a profounder philosophy than our rampaging rhinoceros of scientific naturalism — we need a philosophy which will recognize the absolute reality of things apprehended spiritually, though unseen; a new kind of spiritual realism, which will not deny the reality of the physical world, and will allow ample freedom for science, but will insist that the ultimate meaning of our existence lies in a higher level than the five senses or even the trained intellect can reach. The close connection of these two — a revival of poetry and a new philosophy of spiritual realism — is perfectly obvious. One will support the other, as in ages past, when poetry and philosophy went hand in hand.

So then my thesis is this: we have got too far away from the poetic expression and from the poetic apprehension of religion, bowed down as we are by a mass of facts, scientific and other, which leave us no opportunity for interpretation of their meaning; and we carry over our fact-hunting habit into the realm of religion, to such an extent that we are not interested in anything else. About Joseph, all we care is to establish his date, and find evidence for him in Egyptian inscriptions; whereas, for the purposes of religious teaching, Joseph may be pure fiction — or poetry, I should prefer to say. About our Lord and his gospel, all we care about is the sources of the Gospel tradition, the dates of his birth and death, the length of his ministry, the evidence for his resurrection, and so on. If we could find his tomb, or his manger-cradle, or the carpenter's shop in Nazareth, we would assume that we had proved the credibility of the Gospels "up to the hilt." Meanwhile, spiritual things are spiritually discerned — and unless a fresh poetic awakening follows this war, the spirit of man having been drastically awakened to the full horror of his present way of life as a clever materialist, a shrewd and on the whole an amoral barbarian with his arms full of gadgets and his brain full of facts, trying to live in God's world as if there were no God — unless men are roused out of this waking stupor, and find room in life for imagination, for poetry, for faith, and for idealism, then I fear that not only is religion on the way out of our world, but that all the higher life of mankind will come to a sorry end. We are not a very religious people, really; small wonder that we have little poetry, and that what little there is, is private, recherché, impressionistic, subjective and sentimental. A task of gigantic proportions now lies before us, as a people, as religious people, as a Church! For what does it profit mankind, if victorious armies of mechanists and materialists sweep over the face of the earth? What gain is it if we win a war, only to vulgarize all human society, erecting night clubs where once stood colleges and churches, and releasing radio crooners and swing orchestras to drown out the last echoes of the songs of angels and of poets? No religion — or — church — that has sold its ancient birthright of poetry and imagination, be it ever so orthodox or ever so "modern" in methods, can be expected to do much about *this* problem.

BIBLIOGRAPHY OF THE WRITINGS OF WILLIAM HENRY PAINE HATCH

Compiled by Dr. Hatch

BOOKS

1. *The Pauline Idea of Faith in Its Relation to Jewish and Hellenistic Religion* (Harvard Theological Studies II), Cambridge: Harvard University Press, 1917.

2. *The Gospel Manuscripts of the General Theological Seminary* (Harvard Theological Studies IV), Cambridge: Harvard University Press, 1918. (With Charles Carroll Edmunds.)

3. *The Idea of Faith in Christian Literature from the Death of Saint Paul to the Close of the Second Century*, Strasbourg, 1925.

4. *Greek and Syrian Miniatures in Jerusalem: With an Introduction and a Description of Each of the Seventy-one Miniatures Reproduced* (The Mediaeval Academy of America, Publication No. 6), Cambridge: The Mediaeval Academy of America, 1931.

5. *The Greek Manuscripts of the New Testament at Mount Sinai: Facsimiles and Descriptions* (American Schools of Oriental Research, Publications of the Jerusalem School, Vol. I), Paris: Paul Geuthner, 1932.

6. *The Greek Manuscripts of the New Testament in Jerusalem: Facsimiles and Descriptions* (American Schools of Oriental Research, Publications of the Jerusalem School, Vol II), Paris: Paul Geuthner, 1934.

7. *The 'Western' Text of the Gospels* (The Twenty-third Annual Hale Memorial Sermon, Delivered March 4, 1937), Evanston: Seabury-Western Theological Seminary, 1937.

8. *The Principal Uncial Manuscripts of the New Testament*, Chicago: University of Chicago Press, 1939.

9. *An Album of Dated Syriac Manuscripts*, Boston: The American Academy of Arts and Sciences, 1946.

Articles

1. "Some Illustrations of New Testament Usage from Greek Inscriptions of Asia Minor," *Journal of Biblical Literature*, XXVII (1908), 134–46.

2. "Zur Apostelgeschichte 2, 9," *Zeitschrift für die neutestamentliche Wissenschaft*, IX (1908), 255–56.

3. "The Use of ἀλιτήριος, ἀλιτρός, ἀραῖος, ἐναγής, ἐνθύμιος, παλαμναῖος, and προστρόπαιος; A Study in Greek Lexicography," *Harvard Studies in Classical Philology*, XIX (1908), 157–86.

4. "Note on the Hexameter in James 1 17," *Journal of Biblical Literature*, XXVIII (1909), 149–51.

5. "Ueber den Namen Papias," *Zeitschrift für die neutestamentliche Wissenschaft*, XII (1911), 83.

6. "The Meaning of Acts 1 4," *Journal of Biblical Literature*, XXX (1911), 123–28.

7. "A Manuscript of Jerome's *De Viris Illustribus* belonging to the General Theological Seminary in New York," *Harvard Studies in Classical Philology*, XXIII (1912), 47–69.

8. "A German Apostle of Liberty," *The Christian Register*, XCVI (August 30, 1917), 826.

9. "It is Enough," *The Expositor*, Eighth Series, XV (1918), 157–60.

10. "An Allusion to the Destruction of Jerusalem in the Fourth Gospel," *ibid.*, XVII (1919), 194–97.

11. "A Liberal Churchman's Allegiance to the Creeds," *The Hibbert Journal*, XVII (1919), 716–25.

12. "The Meaning of John XVI, 8–11," *The Harvard Theological Review*, XIV (1921), 103–05.

13. "A Syriac Parallel to the Golden Rule," *ibid.*, 193–95.

14. "The Text of Luke II, 22," *ibid.*, 377–81.

15. "The Road to Bethlehem — A Trip on Donkeyback," *The Churchman*, CXXVI (December 16, 1922), 14–15, 32–33. (Illustrated.)

16. "The Cursing of the Fig Tree," *The Journal of the Palestine Oriental Society*, III (1923), 6–12.

17. "The Scriptures and the Apostles' Creed, with Special Reference to the Birth of Christ," *Creeds and Loyalty: Essays on the History, Interpretation and Use of the Creeds*, By Seven Members of the Faculty of the Episcopal Theological School; New York: Macmillan, 1924, pp. 45–63.

18. "Three Coptic Fragments from Nitria," *The Annual of the American Schools of Oriental Research*, VI (1924–25), 108–11.

19. "A Visit to the Coptic Convents in Nitria," *ibid.*, pp. 93–107.

20. "An Unpublished Greek Inscription from 'Ammân," *ibid.*, VII (1925–26), 100–04.

21. "Three Liturgical Fragments from the Wâdi Natrûn," *ibid.*, pp. 94–99.

22. "A Fragment of a Lost Work on Dioscorus," *The Harvard Theological Review*, XIX (1926), 377–81.

23. "Τὰ στοιχεῖα in Paul and Bardaiṣān," *The Journal of Theological Studies*, XXVIII (1927), 181–82.

24. "The Vulgate, Peshitto, Sahidic, and Bohairic Versions of Acts and the Greek Manuscripts," *The Harvard Theological Review*, XXI (1928), 69–95. (With James Hardy Ropes.)

25. "The Apostles in the New Testament and in the Ecclesiastical Tradition of Egypt," *ibid.*, 147–61.

26. "The Pauline Idea of Forgiveness," *Studies in Early Christianity presented to Frank Chamberlin Porter and Benjamin Wisner Bacon*, edited by Shirley Jackson Case; New York and London: The Century Co., 1928, pp. 335–49.

27. "An Uncial Fragment of the Gospels," *The Harvard Theological Review*, XXIII (1930), 149–52.

28. "What Figure of Christ Emerges from New Testament Criticism?" *Hartford Papers: A Record of the Church Congress in the United States on its Fifty-Eighth Anniversary A.D. MCMXXXII*, With an Introduction by Harold Adye Prichard; Spencer, Mass.: The Heffernan Press, 1932, pp. 135–62.

29. "Six Coptic Fragments of the New Testament from Nitria," *The Harvard Theological Review*, XXVI (1933), 99–108.

30. "The Origin and Meaning of the Term 'Uncial'," *Classical Philology*, XXX (1935), 247–54.

31. "Jesus' Summary of the Law and the Achievement of the Moral Ideal according to St Paul," *Anglican Theological Review*, XVIII (1936), 129–40.

32. "The Position of Hebrews in the Canon of the New Testament," *The Harvard Theological Review*, XXIX (1936), 133–51.

33. "The Subscription in the Chester Beatty Manuscript of the Harclean Gospels," *ibid.*, XXX (1937), 141–55.

34. "A Redating of Two Important Uncial Manuscripts of the Gospels — Codex Zacynthius and Codex Cyprius," *Quantulacumque: Studies Presented to Kirsopp Lake by Pupils, Colleagues and Friends*, London: Christophers, 1937, pp. 333–38.

35. "The Primitive Christian Message," *Journal of Biblical Literature*, LVIII (1939), 1–13. (The Presidential Address, 1938.)

36. "An Early Edition of the New Testament in Greek," *The Harvard Theological Review*, XXXIV (1941), 69–78.

37. "A Note on Matthew 20:15," *Anglican Theological Review*, XXVI (1944), 250–53.

38. "A Note on Matthew 6:33," *The Harvard Theological Review*, XXXVIII (1945), 270–72.

In Preparation

Facsimiles and Descriptions of Minuscule Manuscripts of the New Testament.

"Jesus Christ in the Gospels and in Christian Faith," *The Great Certainty*, edited by W. Bertal Heeney, Toronto, 1946.

"To What Syriac Version or Versions of the Gospels did Thomas of Ḥarqel refer in His Margin," *Journal of Biblical Literature*, LXV (1946).